Mina Loy

Mina Loy

American Modernist Poet

Virginia M. Kouidis

Louisiana State
University Press
Baton Rouge
and London

Mina Loy. Photograph by George Lynes, New York (1938?).
Courtesy of Mrs. Herbert Bayer and Mrs. Fredric Benedict

Design: Albert Crochet
Typeface: VIP Palatino
Composition: G & S Typesetters, Inc.
Printing and binding: Thomson-Shore, Inc.

LIBRARY OF CONGRESS CATALOGING IN PUBLICATION DATA

Kouidis, Virginia M   1943–
    Mina Loy, American modernist poet.
    Bibliography: p.
    Includes index.
    1.   Loy, Mina—Criticism and interpretation. I.   Title.
PS3523.0975Z73   811'.52   80–10661
ISBN 0–8071–0672–0

For Paul

Contents

Illustrations

Acknowledgments

For their assistance in making this book possible I am especially indebted to the American Philosophical Society and the American Civilization Program of the University of Iowa for travel funds; to Sherman Paul, who suggested the study of Mina Loy and then throughout my project gave advice and encouragement, as well as several invaluable readings of the manuscript; and to Mrs. Herbert (Joella) Bayer and Mrs. Fredric (Fabi) Benedict, who graciously shared their memories of their mother and granted me access to her papers. The poems are reprinted here by their permission. For library assistance I want to thank the Interlibrary Loan Department of the University of Iowa Library, Ruth Fourier of the Auburn University Library, and Donald C. Gallup of the Beinecke Rare Book and Manuscript Library, Yale University. I have also been aided by a number of people who have read and criticized my manuscript at various stages of its evolution: Thomas Whitaker, Robert Greene, Robert Corrigan, Alexander Kern, Herbert Leibowitz, and Ward Allen. The English Department of Auburn University has provided the typing services of the patient Frances Henderson and Barbara Fourier; and Julien Levy and Jonathan Williams have kindly responded to my inquiries. Most of all, there is my husband Paul whose encouragement and sound advice have never wavered.

For permission to quote from unpublished sources, I am grateful to these: Mrs. Herbert Bayer and Mrs. Fredric Benedict; the Collection of American Literature, Beinecke Rare Book and Manuscript Library, Yale University. I gratefully acknowledge permission to reprint portions of this study that appeared in *Boundary 2*, III, No. 3.

A Note on the Text

In quoting Mina Loy I have repeatedly faced the dilemma of deciding what irregularity of form, spelling, or punctuation is error, what is innovation. Her writings appeared in little magazines, *Others* anthologies, and Robert McAlmon's Contact Editions, places where the editorial eye was not always alert—to say nothing of the printer's double vision before her typographical experiments. When I have had access to the original manuscripts, I have used them as a guide. Otherwise, I have adhered to the typography and punctuation of the published version of a work. Rather than clutter the text with *sic*, I have corrected misspellings and the misuse of the apostrophe if I thought that I was not altering an intentional play on words or British usage. I have used the same procedure in quoting the letters. Loy often punctuated with dashes and I have retained these because they seem to be part of her typographical experiment and, like irregular spacing, they may be intended to reflect movements of the intellect and intuition. In the poems the dashes and ellipses are her punctuation.

Upon first mention, each poem or prose work is followed by the date of its original publication. When two dates are given, the first indicates the date of composition.

Mina Loy

Prologue

Candidates for the "modern" woman were plentiful in the New York of 1917, but an *Evening Sun* reporter resolved the search for this highly topical figure in the person of Mina Loy, a British-born poet and painter who had come to New York from Florence, Italy, in the fall of 1916. As one of the European expatriates from World War I enlivening the New York art scene, she shared the glamour and notoriety accompanying this group's pursuit of artistic and personal freedom, and with her exceptional beauty, cerebral disposition, and cosmopolitan background, she was one of the most exotic of the artists gathered around avant garde impresarios Alfred Stieglitz, Walter Conrad Arensberg, and Alfred Kreymborg. Within this milieu she distinguished herself, according to the reporter, as a free-verse poet who held "the intuitional pause exactly the right length of time"; a playwright and actress; a designer of lampshades, magazine covers, and clothing; an authority on Italian Futurism; and a painter.[1]

These diverse interests reflect Mina Loy's effort to survive artistically and economically in the twentieth century. Although she undertook them all enthusiastically, painting and poetry were her most enduring interests and achievements—poetry her most substantial claim to modernity. Into poems of personal honesty and daring technical experiment she channeled a hard-won knowledge of self and world that had transformed a Victorian lady into a modern woman and poet whose best poetry ranks her with the leading American modernists. This poetry merits rediscovery because of its contributions to feminist

1. "Do You Strive to Capture the Symbols of Your Reactions? If Not You Are Quite Old Fashioned," New York *Evening Sun*, February 13, 1917, p. 10.

thought and art and to an understanding of the origins, practice, and aims of American poetic modernism. But, most important, the poetry merits attention because of its daring and frequently successful attempt to make language reflect the movement of consciousness in a world of constant change and vague purpose.

Ezra Pound, one of the first to commend Loy's poetry and recognize its contributions to the American poetry revolution, crowed from London in 1918: "Mi credo, Masters, Frost, Lindsay are out of the Wild Young American gaze already. Williams, Loy, Moore, and the worser phenomena of *Others* . . . are much more in the 'news.'" A more subdued letter (1921) to Marianne Moore addressed the same issue: "Entre nooz: is there anyone in America except you, Bill and Mina Loy who can write anything of interest in verse?"[2] Literary history, following Pound's lead, has acknowledged the affinity, in tendency if not in quality, and remembers Mina Loy, when it has bothered to remember, as an American modernist poet.

I

The modernist credentials Mina Loy presented to her American hosts were impressive. She was born in London, December 27, 1882, into a prosperous English middle-class family, the oldest of three daughters. Her father's family were Hungarian Jews; her mother's English Protestant. Although women in this culture received little formal education, the father, Sigmund Lowy, pampered his talented daughter and sent her at seventeen to Munich to study art with Angelo Jank. Later she studied art in Paris, and at one time, probably between her trips to Munich and Paris, she was a student of Augustus John in England. These student days she recalled for her friend Carl Van Vechten:

> There is very little to say about Paris—all the drawing I ever learnt was with Angelo Jank in Munich—and I used to take my fantasy

2. D. D. Paige (ed.), *The Letters of Ezra Pound, 1907–1941* (New York: Harcourt, Brace & World, 1950), 135–36, 168.

drawings to Dasio's class—who always proclaimed me a genius and told the other poor women to look at this "and go home and darn——["] These appreciations I found in art-schools—used to frighten me—for I never knew how I did anything—and then I began to wonder if I could manage to do it again—and couldn't work for a month—Primet at Calarossis was the only master in Paris that made a fuss of my work—But Paris in those days for everyone meant just learning to love the dear old impressionists—I had Manet and Monet on the spot—but Degas frightened me for a year—and I shall always feel grateful to the day I first "*saw*" the early Renoirs—But the most beautiful things in Paris were the Fêtes—and the Bal Bullier.[3]

During these years she shortened her family name, Mina Gertrude Lowy, to Mina Loy; and in Paris she met and married (December 31, 1903) Stephen Haweis (Hugh Oscar William Haweis), an English painter and a member of a family of distinguished Episcopalian ministers. The Haweises had three children: Ada Janet (1904–1905), Joella Synara (b. 1907), and Giles (1909–1923).

Mina Loy and her husband were both involved in the early-century revolution in painting. A review of the 1906 Salon d'Automne records their presence: M. Haweis "pur whistlérien," and "Mlle Mina Loy qui, dans ses singulières aquarelles où se combinent Guys, Rops et Beardsley, nous montre des éphèbes ambigus dont la nudité est choyée par des dames en falbalas de 1885."[4] Van Vechten vividly describes a similar painting: "One day on the beach at the Lido she saw a young man in a bathing suit lying stretched on the sand with his head in the lap of a beautiful woman. Other women surrounded the two. The group im-

3. Mina Loy to Carl Van Vechten, *ca.* summer, 1915, in Collection of American Literature, Beinecke Rare Book and Manuscript Library, Yale University. Hereinafter letters to Van Vechten, all in the Beinecke, will not be footnoted; significant dates will be cited in the text.

4. Paul Jamot, "Le Salon d'Automne," *Gazette des Beaux-Arts*, 3rd ser., XXXVI (1906), 484. Mr. Haweis, "pure Whistler," and "Miss Mina Loy who, in her strange watercolors where are combined Guy, Rops and Beardsley, shows us ambiguous ephebes whose nudity is caressed by ladies in the furbelows of 1885."

mediately suggested a composition to her. She went home and painted. She took the young man's bathing suit off and the women she dressed in lovely floating robes, and she called the picture *L'Amour Dorloté par les Belles Dames.*"[5] (Following page 48.) The eroticism, ephebes, and costume place Mina Loy among the Decadent painters rather than the more revolutionary Post-impressionists. However the descriptions also suggest that Mina Loy was a critic of the Decadence, approaching her subject with the irony that shaped her later poetic satires of the Decadents. Another painting, described by Mabel Dodge, a friend, discloses one of several tragedies in Mina Loy's life: "The night . . . [her] little daughter died, she sat up all night and made the extraordinary tempera painting called 'The Wooden Madonna' that I still have: the foolish-looking mother holding her baby, whose two small fingers are raised in an impotent blessing over the other anguished mother who, on her knees, curses them both with great, upraised, clenched fists, and her own baby sprawling dead with little arms and legs outstretched lifeless, like faded flower petals."[6]

Whether the Haweises were as much a part of Parisian artistic life as Mina Loy was to be in the 1920s is unknown. Her acquaintance with Guillaume Apollinaire as well as her friendship with Gertrude Stein may date from this time. Perhaps Mina was still too much the English lady to have been extensively involved in bohemian circles. She writes to Van Vechten (*ca.* 1915): "When I was twenty-three I was elected a member of the Autumn Salon and then I stole away from civilization—to live on the Costa San Giorgio." Although she speaks of it as a refuge, the life Mina Loy escaped to in Florence from 1907 to 1916 continued her modernist education.

In Florence the Haweises seem to have met Mabel Dodge and

5. Carl Van Vechten, "An Interrupted Conversation," *Rogue*, I (February 1, 1915), 14.

6. Mabel Dodge Luhan, *Intimate Memories*, Vol. II: *European Experiences* (New York: Harcourt Brace, 1935), 340–41.

become part of her circle at the Villa Curonia, and it was probably at the Villa Curonia that Mina (then known as "Dusie," or
"Ducie," because she confused the German pronouns "du" and
"sie") met Van Vechten in 1913. He has left a colorful sketch of
his close friend, a lovely woman strikingly elegant on the dusty
streets of a vacation retreat near Vallombrosa:

> She made an unforgettable figure with her gray-blue eyes, her patri-
> cian features, her waved black hair, parted in the centre. Tall and
> slender, her too large ankles were concealed by the tight hobble-
> skirts she wore. Her dresses, of soft dove-coloured shades, or bril-
> liant lemon with magenta flowers, or pale green and blue, were ex-
> tremely lovely. Strange, long earrings dangled from her artificially
> rosy ears: one amber pair imprisoned flies with extended wings. It is
> easy to recall Ducie as she tramped along the dusty roads of Vallom-
> brosa, enveloped in a brown cloak trimmed with variegated fur,
> scarcely able, thanks to her tight skirts, to move one smartly shod
> foot in front of the other.[7]

The Haweises also knew the English community in Florence;
and they entertained Gertrude Stein, who had a summer villa
near Florence, and read *The Making of Americans* in manuscript.
Stephen Haweis requested the addition of commas, but Mina
earned the appreciation from Miss Stein that "Mina Loy . . .
was able to understand without the commas. She has always
been able to understand."[8]

By 1913 Mina's marriage to Haweis was disintegrating, and
Mabel Dodge says that even in their art-student days their marriage had been stormy. Mina's letters indicate that she suffered
from what she thought was his unfaithfulness, and she was sick
for long periods with influenza, nerves, and headaches—a condition perhaps best characterized as neurasthenia. Mabel Dodge
draws a rather unkind portrait of the couple and their incompatibility. Stephen was a *"penguin* type" who fascinated numer-

7. Carl Van Vechten, *Sacred and Profane Memories* (London: Cassell, 1932), 130.
8. Gertrude Stein, *The Autobiography of Alice B. Toklas* (New York: Random
House, 1960), 132.

ous women: "diminutive, black as a beetle, and very, very inky.
. . . His dark, inky eyes would have an oily glint in them and his
long black hair that grew, like a page's, long and over his ears,
used to grow damp and he would brush it back with his trem-
bling lizardy hands. . . . He was very *fin-de-siècle* and sad." Of
the pair, Mrs. Dodge writes: "Stephen and Ducie Haweis were a
strange couple together. She was beautiful, with dark hair
parted and with a great knot on the nape of her white neck, a
fair, fine skin with high cheekbones, and she was graceful." But
the description is tainted: "She looked like a painting by Augustus John. Her eyes were long and narrow of a nondescript
color, something pale. There was something a little reptilian
about her, too. Just as Stephen resembled a lizard or a little tor-
toise on end, so she made one think of serpents. Lilith her name
might have been." Both were dissatisfied, and he would com-
plain, says Mrs. Dodge, "about wanting love, and about wanting to be understood." Mina "seemed to grow dry as the years
went on."[9]

Mina Loy was fairly hard on herself. In a biographical sketch
(*ca.* 1915), intended probably for Van Vechten's article "Some
'Literary Ladies' I Have Known," she characterizes her life as
one "of shilly-shallying shyness—of an utter inability to adjust
myself to anything actual," and she describes herself as "a sort
of hermit crab occasionally lured to expansiveness under the
luxury of Mabel Dodge's flowering trees." She says, perhaps
with some exaggeration, for Joella remembers that her mother
had servants in Florence, that her "conceptions of Life have
evolved while I have been stirring baby food on spirit lamps—
and my best drawings behind a stove to the accompaniment of a
line of children's cloths hanging round it to dry—I have seen
very little of what is going on—and often when I have been led
forth from the wilds by a friend I have only marvelled at the

9. Luhan, *Intimate Memories*, 337–41.

paucity of the human imagination." The exceptions had been "a few Picassos—Wyndham Lewis—and Nijinski dancing—Perfection is infrequent. I *have* gasped too at a picture of Carrà's and of course the shattering beauty, Marinetti's readings of Futurist poems—and at the inebriation of early Papini in Un Uomo Finito. And the sublime epics of the commonplace made by Arnold Bennett—and the eyes of a tuberculous beggar on the Via Tornabuoni—and a line I picked up of Laforgue's."

The Florence years, although brightened by occasional meetings with artistic excellence—the conversation at Mabel Dodge's villa, visits to England, and exhibits there of her painting—were indeed full of personal problems. In addition to her own ill health Mina faced two-year-old Joella's affliction by polio and, in response, adopted a nontraditional form of Christian Science, a religion of positive thinking forecasting the secular religion of selfhood she was soon to set forth in her poetry. She also had financial worries, worries intensified when Haweis left for Australia and the South Seas, via New York and the Bahamas, in 1913. Her letters to Van Vechten and Mabel Dodge, both now in New York, express her fear that Haweis is discrediting her with their mutual friends. She is also trying to enlist Van Vechten's aid in obtaining a divorce, fearful that Haweis will not cooperate in the divorce proceedings and offend her family in a scandal.

Futurism seems to have temporarily reinforced Christian Science to provide the spiritual strength with which Mina Loy met these crises. She knew the Futurists by 1913, and while they may have compounded her personal problems they also gave her the psychic energy to turn some of her difficulties into art. Her daughter recalls that Carlo Carrà, and, very occasionally, Filippo Marinetti and Giovanni Papini were guests at her mother's house, and in early 1914 Mina writes to Mabel Dodge: "I am in the throes of conversion to Futurism—but I shall never convince myself—There is no hope in any system that 'combat le mal avec le mal' . . . and that is really Marinetti's philosophy." [10] She elaborates her antipathy to the martial aspects of Futurism in *Psycho-Democracy* (1917/1920), a prose answer to Marinetti's *War, the World's Only Hygiene* (1911–1915). But whatever her reservations about the Futurist program, she says in the same letter that Marinetti "is one of the most satisfying personalities I ever came in contact with." In letters to Van Vechten she credits Marinetti with "waking me up"; he taught her, she says, how to use her "vitality." Mina Loy probably had affairs with Marinetti and Papini; she was in love with Papini. These romantic involvements were short-lived and painful for Mina, who transformed her bitterness into poetic satire.

During this time Mina Loy's poetry began to appear. Distinctly feminine in its exploration of female oppression, the poetry seems Futurist inspired in its aggressive assertion of selfhood and in its structural experiment. Futurism also enters specifically into the subject matter of several poems. "Aphorisms on Futurism" (1914), the first modernist credentials she sent to America, outline a program of psychic fulfillment; but "Lions' Jaws" (1920) attacks Futurism as an insincere art movement that has turned art into a circus. The Futurists are dubbed "flabbergasts" and "Raminetti" is Marinetti, a circus-master:

> astride a prismatic locomotive
> ramping the tottering platform
> of the Arts
> of which this conjuring commercial traveller
> imported some novelties from
> Paris in his pocket . . .
> souvenirs for his disciples
> to flaunt
> at his dynamic carnival

10. Mina Loy to Mabel Dodge, February, 1914, in Collection of American Literature, Beinecke Rare Book and Manuscript Library, Yale University. Hereinafter letters to Mrs. Dodge, all in the Beinecke, will not be footnoted; significant dates will be cited in the text.

But she also mocks her own illusion that she was the exception to Futurist contempt for women; these "amusing" men needed no muse:

> These amusing men
> discover in their mail
> duplicate petitions
> to be the lurid mother of "their" flabbergast child
> from Nima Lyo, alias Anim Yol, alias
> Imna Oly
> (secret service buffoon to the Woman's Cause)

II

During her later years in Florence Mina Loy wanted to see New York. She would tell the *Evening Sun* reporter that one had to live in New York before qualifying as an inhabitant of the "Modern world," and she saw herself as a Columbus drawn to the emerging center of the present, like him to be discovered by America. She remained in Florence during the beginning of World War I and was caught up in Futurist enthusiasm for the war, working for a while as a nurse in a surgical hospital. But she was soon disillusioned with the war and distracted by personal problems. She was seeking a divorce from Haweis and needed money. Perhaps New York would provide a market for her dress designs.

She came alone to New York in the fall of 1916, expecting her children, left with a nurse in Florence, to join her when she was settled. While New York did not provide financial improvement, it did supply a community of like-minded artists and bring a moment of personal happiness. Among the city's expatriates she met Arthur Cravan (Fabian Avenarius Lloyd), a nephew of Oscar Wilde, world vagabond, and Dadaist forerunner who defied the conventional world's absurdities and inhibitions with a thoroughness and bravado that Mina admired but could not emulate. A note in her unpublished papers gives her assessment of Cravan:

Led hallucinatory life of destitute world-tramp, in challenge of "la bêtise humaine."

His slogan "On ne me fait marcher moi."

Unique phenomenon, a biological mystic he traced his poetic sensibility to his power to "think" with any part of his body. His poetry reveals a physical illumination detonating as gun-cotton.

Conscious, in adolescence, of his phenomenal strength alone, when later his intellectual faculties came into play the instinct of "knock out" dominated his critique. Throughout the most distressing circumstances his abnormal capacity for enjoyment to the exclusion of other reactions subsisted intact. His gesture of destiny was "Samson upsetting the temple." [11]

Cravan's biographer Bernard Delvaille substantiates this assessment, seeing in Cravan a sensitive man who used his humor and nonconformity as a mask, a view he documents with Cravan's own self-estimate: "'Je suis brute à me donner un coup de poing dans les dents et subtil jusqu' à la neurasthénie.'" [12] Born to an English couple in Lausanne in 1887, Cravan developed the nonconformity that forced him out of several schools, and at seventeen he left for the United States where he worked his way to California as a chauffeur, boxer, orange picker, and lumberjack. Upon his return to Europe he went to Berlin and lived among the city's lowlife, its homosexuals, prostitutes, thieves, drug addicts, and gamblers. By 1909 he was in Paris combating his boredom with Parisian literary life in a series of antics that helped to create the legend that made him and Jacques Vaché, according to the historian Maurice Nadeau, "two meteors, two fixed stars in the surrealist firmament." [13] His nonconformist gestures included an assault upon Mme Delaunay for which he served eight days in jail, insults to Apollinaire and Marie Lau-

11. Mina Loy, Note (in possession of Mrs. Herbert Bayer, Montecito, California).

12. Bernard Delvaille, Preface to *Maintenant* by Arthur Cravan, ed. Bernard Delvaille (Paris: Erik Losfeld [1957]), 9–11. "I am beastly enough to give myself a blow in the teeth and subtle to the point of neurasthenia."

13. Maurice Nadeau, *History of Surrealism*, trans. Richard Howard (New York: Macmillan, 1965), 55.

rencin that provoked Apollinaire to a duel, and an insulting interview with André Gide. He also drew attention to himself by marketing his one-man publication *Maintenant* from a wheelbarrow. When the war broke out he fled to Spain to escape conscription. There he earned passage to New York by fighting former world heavyweight champion Jack Johnson, going three rounds before Johnson knocked him out.[14] In New York Cravan's most notorious impropriety was an attempt to disrobe during a lecture he was delivering on modern humor at the New York Independents Exhibition.[15]

Mina Loy, seeing more than the clown, found in Cravan the answer to a question she had put to Van Vechten before she came to New York: "Do you think there is a man in America one *could* love." They were married in Mexico City in January, 1918 (she had been divorced from Haweis in 1917). Cravan prospected for silver, opened a boxing school, and prepared a lecture on Egyptian art.[16] Recalling her time in Mexico for Mabel Dodge (1920), Mina wrote that she was disappointed in herself for not working: "I had too many other things to think of there—and I find my memory not quite clear enough to do anything really substantial of it. I have never found such subjects as some of the unexpected eyes of beggars." The typescript of the novel "Colossus," based on Mina's relationship with Cravan, describes the newlyweds as starving in Mexico until they are rescued by a couple of English visitors.[17] The Mexican interlude, idyll or nightmare, ended with Cravan's disappearance in October,

14. Delvaille, Preface to *Maintenant*, 13–14; Roger Shattuck, *The Banquet Years: The Origins of the Avant-Garde in France—1885 to World War I* (New York: Random House, 1968), 286, 353–54.

15. André Breton, "Caractères de l'evolution moderne," in *Les Pas perdus*, quoted by Nadeau, *History of Surrealism*, 55; Gabrielle Buffet-Picabia, "Arthur Cravan and American Dada" (1938), in Robert Motherwell (ed.), *The Dada Painters and Poets: An Anthology* (New York: George Wittenborn, 1951), 13–17.

16. Delvaille, Preface to *Maintenant*, 14.

17. Mina Loy, "Colossus" (Typescript in possession of Mrs. Herbert Bayer, Montecito, California).

1918. Mina had preceded him to Buenos Aires and Rio de Jan-
iero where he was to join her, but he never arrived. Legend has
it that he was last seen alive boarding a boat on the Mexican
coast.

After Cravan's disappearance and the birth of their daughter
Jemima Fabienne (Fabi) in April, 1919, Mina Loy searched for
her missing husband in Europe and America. Eventually she
learned from the U.S. State Department that his body had been
found beaten and robbed in the Mexican desert. She eulogized
her love in "The Widow's Jazz" (1931), in which Negro jazz
rhythms evoke memories of the dead husband:

> Cravan
> colossal absentee
> the substitute dark
> rolls to the incandescent memory
>
> of love's survivor
> on this rich suttee
>
> seared by the flames of sound
> the widowed urn
>
> holds impotently
> your murdered laughter
>
> Husband
> how secretly you cuckold me with death

The depth of her loss appears also in her response to the *Little
Review* "Questionnaire" of 1929: "What has been the happiest
moment of your life?"—"Every moment I spent with Arthur
Cravan." "The unhappiest?"—"The rest of the time."

III

In terms of her poetry the New York years boded the possibility
that Mina Loy might, as Pound guessed, emerge from the confused nebula of artistic experiment to become one of the lumi-
naries of American modernism. New York's little magazines

seem to have provided the first and only outlet for her poetry until 1920. She was still in Europe when her work began to appear, in 1914, in several New York magazines—*Camera Work, Trend, International, Rogue,* and *Others,* magazines vital to the first stages of America's awakened poetic consciousness. Her principal channel seems to have been Carl Van Vechten. He knew Pitts Sanborn, editor of *Trend* (1911–1915), and he himself edited the last few issues, dedicating them to the exclusion of "'stupidity, banality, cant, clap-trap morality, Robert W. Chambersism, sensationalism for its own sake.'"[18] The *Rogue,* a Londonish 1890s magazine edited by Louise and Allen Norton in Greenwich Village (1915–1916), published Van Vechten, Walter Conrad Arensberg, Wallace Stevens, and Donald Evans— writers attempting to succeed the Decadents.[19] Alfred Stieglitz' *Camera Work* (1903–1919), which had long served to introduce a few Americans to the latest European artistic and literary movements, printed Mina Loy's "Aphorisms on Futurism." But her association with *Others* (1915–1919) was most important. This magazine, begun by Arensberg and Alfred Kreymborg, explained its purpose in its name. According to its epigraph, "The old expressions are with us always, / And there are always others." "Old expressions" refers to the nineteenth-century poetic attitudes and techniques that still dominated the established literary magazines. Some of the *Others* poets also resented Harriet Monroe's *Poetry,* a little magazine founded in 1912 that encouraged the Chicago renaissance and brought Lindsay, Masters, and Sandburg to the public's attention. Under Ezra Pound's influence it supported Imagism. Many of the experimentalists, quickly moving beyond Imagism, felt rejected by Miss Monroe and turned to *Others,* a magazine so open to innovation that

18. Bruce Kellner, *Carl Van Vechten and the Irreverent Decades* (Norman: University of Oklahoma Press, 1968), 87.
19. Carl Van Vechten, "Rogue Elephant in Porcelain" (*ca.* 1914), *Yale University Library Gazette,* XXXVIII (1963), 41–50.

William Carlos Williams, one of its most experimental poets, faulted its lack of critical standards.[20] In its brief existence *Others* printed most of the pioneer American modernists. Williams, Wallace Stevens, T. S. Eliot, Marianne Moore, and Ezra Pound shared its pages with lesser poets, many of whom never rose above their original obscurity.

Mina Loy, like many of her contemporaries, needed *Others*. During the decade 1910–1920 the major outlets for her poems were *Others* magazine and anthologies (published by Kreymborg in 1916, 1917, and 1920). She was a mutual choice of Arensberg and Kreymborg for the first issue of the magazine, contributing the startlingly erotic, technically difficult *Love Songs*, a four-poem collage, later expanded to thirty-four poems, presenting a disillusioned and cynical analysis of religious and romantic love. Even Kreymborg had difficulties with Mina Loy's poetry, and a public generally confused by the magazine directed its resentment at Loy and Orrick Johns, whose "Olives," parodies of Kreymborg's "Mushrooms," were rhythmless short lyrics on life's trivia. The verse of Loy and Johns earned *Others* the scurrilous title "the little yellow dog," a reference both to its yellow cover and the remnants of the Decadence in some of its poems.[21]

While America provided an outlet for Mina Loy's poems, she fed the desire of the Americans to learn more of European revolutions in art. Her contributions to their experiments suggest ideas and aesthetics derived from the *fin de siècle*, Jules Laforgue, Henri Bergson, and Futurism. These artistic sources combined with a sense of feminine oppression to shape Mina Loy into one

20. William Carlos Williams, *The Autobiography* (New York: New Directions, 1951), 141–42.

21. Alfred Kreymborg, *Troubadour: An Autobiography* (New York: Boni and Liveright, 1925), 221–23, 235; Alfred Kreymborg, *A History of American Poetry: Our Singing Strength* (New York: Tudor, 1934), 488–89; and René Taupin, *L'Influence du Symbolisme Français sur la Poésie Américaine, de 1910 à 1920* (Paris: Librairie Ancienne Honoré Champion, 1929), 265–66.

of the most radical avant garde poets. Later readers were to understand her unconventionality as proto-Surrealist; but when her poetry first appeared, its free-verse presentation of human absurdity and sexual and psychic frustration confused and shocked traditionalists.

Her place within New York's avant garde is explained by William Carlos Williams in the Prologue to *Kora in Hell* (1920). He distinguishes between two poles of artistic activity: the North of Marianne Moore who fastidiously˚ avoided everything she "detested"; the South of Mina Loy and her associates who, Williams implies, tolerated innovation tinted with the absurd, the obscene, the nihilistic.[22] His case in point is Loy's participation in the *Blind Man*, an ephemeral (April and May, 1917) little magazine with Dada leanings which focused its advocacy of artistic freedom first on the Independents exhibition of 1917 and then on the exclusion from the exhibit of Marcel Duchamp's ready-made sculpture "La Fontaine," a urinal signed "R. Mutt." Loy wrote no poetry for the magazine but helped to set its tone with a defense of the artist's unique vision, a verbal montage of avant garde social life, and an appreciation of the painter Louis M. Eilshemius.

Another American forum for Mina Loy was the Provincetown Theatre, an important element in the modernist ferment. She was one of numerous writers and artists who formed the periphery of the Provincetown in its early days. And in December, 1916, she joined with William Carlos Williams and Bill Zorach to perform Kreymborg's *Lima Beans*—a successful one-act amateur production, according to its author who recalled "the supersophisticated Mina sniffing a little at the commonplaceness of the marriage theme. . . . The part of the wife—much too light for a person of Mina's worldly experience—nevertheless ap-

22. William Carlos Williams, "Prologue to *Kora in Hell*" (1920), in *Selected Essays of William Carlos Williams* (New York: New Directions, 1954), 7.

pealed to her sense of comedy and she grew closer to the character with each rehearsal."[23] During a second visit to New York in the early 1920s she again appeared on the Provincetown stage, under the pseudonym Imna Oly, as "Esther, a spinster" in Lawrence Vail's *What D'You Want* (December 27, 1920).[24]

Besides acting she also wrote experimental plays. Two very short plays of the Italian years, "Collision" and "Cittàbapini" (1915), seem efforts at the creation of Futurist movement and surrealistic image. "The Sacred Prostitute" (*ca.* 1914, unpublished) concerns the Futurists. Set in the "World Brothel," it satirizes male attitudes toward women: Don Juans, "Idealists," and "Tea-Table men" as well as the Futurists.[25] "The Pamperers" (*ca.* 1916) initiated the short-lived "Modern Forms" section of the *Dial* (July, 1920), which was "devoted to exposition and consideration of the less traditional types of art." Mina Loy's knowledge of avant garde movements was the source of this satire on artistic movements in general, grouped under the label "Vitalism." Employing one of her favorite themes, the play mocks the insincere disciples of art: aesthetes, modern women, and the easily corrupted artistic "genius."

Mina Loy's person provoked almost as much interest among her associates as did her numerous talents. She was a striking woman, with her friend Djuna Barnes one of the most attractive figures of the New York avant garde world. Man Ray remembered them as "stunning subjects" for his camera, "one in light tan clothes of her own design, the other all in black with a veil."[26] She was also an excellent conversationalist, prized in a group that fed upon discussion. She was at home with the paradoxical *Rogue* conversationalists who gathered around Arens-

23. Kreymborg, *Troubadour*, 309.
24. See Helen Deutsch and Stella Hanou, *The Provincetown: A Story of the Theatre* (New York: Farrar & Rinehart, 1931), 31, 51, 204, 243.
25. Mina Loy, "The Sacred Prostitute" (MS in Collection of American Literature, Beinecke Rare Book and Manuscript Library, Yale University).
26. Man Ray, *Self Portrait* (London: Andre Deutsch, 1963), 98.

berg,[27] and she joined the *Others* contributors for picnics at Grantwood, New Jersey, where excited debates about Cubism often occupied a Sunday afternoon.[28]

In the twenties Mina Loy's search for news of Cravan took her back to New York and a brief residence in Greenwich Village. This period of her life is touched upon in Robert McAlmon's *Post-Adolescence: 1920–1921* (1923). She is "Gusta Rolph," characteristically cynical about men:

> "I'll have to use that in my book on men; just another idea for showing up what a sham he is," Gusta stated, appearing animated now that many people were about. "What tricks men play on us doting women."
>
> "You know, Gusta, you like the darlings too well to do them the harsh justice they need," Brander [Marsden Hartley] told her.
>
> "Don't destroy my inspiration. I must do something, even if it's only trying to be clever," Gusta said, giving an impression of the real discouragement, almost despair, behind her trifling.[29]

IV

After leaving New York Mina traveled with her daughters in Austria and Berlin (Haweis had returned in 1916 and taken their son). Through *Dial* editor Scofield Thayer she met Freud, who read her short stories and pronounced them analytical. She finally came to rest in Paris in 1923. For a while Joella attended the Elizabeth Duncan school of dance, but she returned to comfort her mother when Giles died in 1923.

27. Kreymborg, *Troubadour*, 219–20.
28. See Williams, *The Autobiography*, 135–36. Bram Dijkstra, *The Hieroglyphics of a New Speech: Cubism, Stieglitz, and the Early Poetry of William Carlos Williams* (Princeton: Princeton University Press, 1969), 3–46, discusses the New York avant garde circles in which Mina Loy moved, as does Dickran Tashjian, *Skyscraper Primitives: Dada and the American Avant-Garde, 1910–1925* (Middleton, Conn.: Wesleyan University Press, 1975). Although Tashjian mentions Loy only in passing, he provides useful background for her life and art and he gives extended attention to Arthur Cravan.
29. Robert E. Knoll (ed.), *McAlmon and the Lost Generation: A Self-Portrait* (Lincoln: University of Nebraska Press, 1962), 136.

Uneducated to self-support, Mina struggled to provide for her family. Describing herself as "poor" and so ridden by "daily anxiety" that she couldn't do the creative work "bursting for expression," she appealed to Mable Dodge (*ca.* 1921) for assistance in opening a restaurant in Paris. This scheme seems never to have materialized, but Mina was finally able to turn her artistic talent to profit. She had been noted in the New York years for her clothing and lampshade designs, and in 1923 Peggy Guggenheim opened a Paris shop for her in which she marketed her lampshade creations. Sixteen-year-old Joella managed the business and Mina furnished the designs, many of them "firsts"— such as the use of bottles, globes, and decorated clear plastic for lampshades. The shop was fairly successful but any satisfaction Mina may have felt was marred by her obsessive fear that her designs were being stolen. Joella recalls as typical of her mother's inclination to do things in the most difficult way the decision to decorate the shop by rubbing lead dust into the walls. The effect with the lamps was lovely, but it was a messy and difficult task for Joella, the one assigned to carry it out.

Socially Mina Loy was at the heart of the excitement of the twenties. Her friends form a distinguished "Who's Who" of Paris 1920–1930: André Gide, Paul Valéry, Gertrude Stein (and Alice Toklas), Peggy Guggenheim, Colette, Robert McAlmon, Ernest Hemingway, Sylvia Beach, Adrienne Monnier, James Joyce, Constantin Brancusi, Djuna Barnes, and Natalie Barney. She was also a hostess to American expatriates and visitors;[30] and Americans such as Robert McAlmon and Glenway Wescott were able to obtain introductions to Miss Stein's salon through Mina Loy.[31] Harriet Monroe, one of the more sedate American visitors, met Mina in 1923. Although she couldn't resist the temptation to punctuate Mina's poetry, Miss Monroe found

30. Robert McAlmon, *Being Geniuses Together, 1920–1930*, ed. Kay Boyle (Garden City, N.Y.: Doubleday, 1968), 38.
31. Stein, *The Autobiography*, 200.

nothing lacking in the woman herself. Of a gathering of McAlmon, Ezra Pound, Jane Heap, Tristan Tzara, and others at a Paris cafe, Miss Monroe wrote: "Perhaps a great deal of this gayety and color aforesaid was due to the presence of Mina Loy. I may never have fallen very hard for this lady's poetry, but her personality is quite irresistible. Beauty ever-young which has survived four babies, and charm which will survive a century if she lives that long, are sustained by a gayety that seems the worldly-wise conquest of many despairs—all expressed in a voice which, as someone said of Masefield's is 'rich with all the sorrows of the world.' Yes, poetry is in this lady whether she writes it or not." [32]

Most memoirs are likely to include Mina Loy as present at the decade's famous "happenings"—for instance, a reading by Joyce at Sylvia Beach's bookshop, the performance of Ezra Pound's opera, or the supper for Mr. and Mrs. William Carlos Williams, another set of American visitors, at the Trianon, Joyce's favorite restaurant. McAlmon in *Being Geniuses Together* finds the Paris bars and cafes enhanced by the company of his lovely friends Mina Loy and Djuna Barnes.

Within this lively milieu Mina gave her daughters a unique education in cosmopolitan artistic and social life. She included them in many of her activities, and mother and daughters were frequently remarked in the Paris art scene. According to Sylvia Beach,

> We had three raving beauties in "the Crowd," all in one family, which was not fair. Mina Loy, the poetess, and her daughters, Joella and Faby . . . were so lovely that they were stared at wherever they went, and were used to it. But I believe if a vote had been taken, Mina would have been elected the most beautiful of the three. Joyce, who could see as well as anyone when he wanted to, observed that Joella was a beauty according to all the standards: her golden hair, her eyes, her complexion, her manners. So she had Joyce's vote. Faby, still a

32. H[arriet] M[onroe], "The Editor in France," *Poetry*, XXIII (1923), 95–96.

little girl, but beautiful, was very interesting looking. One couldn't keep one's eyes off her.[33]

Experiences with the avant garde were so routine for the children that their memories seem humorously unappreciative: for Joella, the company of interesting but older people when she wanted to be with young men; for Fabi, the necessity of returning early from school on Thursdays to clean and to serve lemonade at her mother's weekly receptions. The girls learned social ease from their mother as well as contempt for all things bourgeois and the rule of thumb that one's attire should be a mark of differentiation. (Ironically, the liberated poet of the *Love Songs* upheld marriage as the ideal for her daughters, wanting them happily married but then resenting their attention to their husbands.)

The early twenties also mark the maturing of Mina Loy's poetry. With *Others* dead, the *Dial* and the *Little Review* sponsored many *Others* alumni. The *Dial* especially was concerned with publishing highly finished literary and artistic works. Several of Loy's best poems were published in the magazine, along with two water colors and a drawing. The poem "Brancusi's Golden Bird," accompanied by a photograph of the sculpture, was included in the famous *Dial* of November, 1922: *The Waste Land* had the position of honor in the format, and Robert Delaunay's painting *Saint-Sévérin* underscored Eliot's dissolution of traditional forms. Loy's poem stands up well among these masterpieces of modern art; its own achievement and praise of abstract form mark her emergence from the exploratory previous decade when her poetry, too, involved itself in chaos. Loy's contributions to the *Little Review* included the Futurist-inspired *Psycho-Democracy* and "Lions' Jaws," and the first installments of the semi-autobiographical *Anglo-Mongrels and the Rose* (1923–1924).

33. Sylvia Beach, *Shakespeare and Company* (New York: Harcourt Brace & World, 1959), 113.

Robert McAlmon published her collection of poems, *Lunar Baedeker*, in 1923 (the original misspelling of *Baedecker* is usually attributed to McAlmon); and he included the last half of *Anglo-Mongrels* in his *Contact Collection of Contemporary Writers* (1925). But after the Contact publications Mina Loy did not make significant advances in her art or public. Her personal life is veiled in mystery, but a lingering neurasthenia and a lack of discipline probably undermined the potential for poetic greatness indicated by the poetry of the early twenties. She continued to write almost to her death but seldom with the daring structural innovations and stunning diction that characterize the poems of 1913–1925.

When the twenties ended Mina Loy faded from public view. The "Questionnaire" with which the *Little Review* ceased publication in 1929 was one indication of the era's demise, and the inclusion of Loy's response signaled her own departure from the shrinking literary and social milieu whose dynamism had aided her in attaining minor recognition. In Paris until December, 1936, living in the same apartment building as her friend Djuna Barnes, she occasionally recaptured, as a letter to Van Vechten (December, 1934) indicates, some of the previous decade's gaiety: "(Chirico tells me the end of the world is being postponed but I send this just the same.) Paris waiting for this end of the world has become hot out of season and ominously dark. I dash about the Champs Elysee with Brancusi—who is impregnated with marble dust—looking for a little buoyancy—we found it 'all' in 'The Thin Man'—and decided to leave instantly for America— But at the door there was only a taxi—and I had no wings." Joella married art dealer Julien Levy in 1927 and moved to New York. Fabi remained with her mother until Christmas, 1935, when she too went to New York. A year later Mina followed her daughters. Living with Joella, who was recently separated from her husband and trying to care for and support three children, Mina (now fifty-four) had become increasingly hard to please, unable to adjust her schedule to the needs of a young family. Her compassion and understanding were, it seems, channeled into her poetry, for in her life she was often indifferent or blind to the needs and feelings of others.

V

Except for a poem in Kreymborg's *Lyric America* (1930) and two poems in *Pagany* (1931), an eleven-year public silence followed *Anglo-Mongrels and the Rose*. But Mina Loy did continue to write. Her most complete effort was the unpublished novel "Insel," a presentation of the Surrealist personality and the narrator's reaction to it.[34] The title character is based on the German Surrealist painter Oelze, whom Mina knew in Paris in the 1930s and tried to help with what she thought was a drug problem. She also continued to paint, and her son-in-law Julien Levy exhibited her paintings in his New York gallery in 1933. He remembers that they "consisted of monochrome sand paintings on paper (a process Mina 'invented' and which resembled fresco). The color was a grey-blue and the subject her personal 'angels' (rather like Blake in spirit)."[35]

In the early 1940s her interest returned to poetry. Numerous poems in her files carry dates for the years 1942–1945, and in 1946 and 1947 four poems appeared in *Accent*. These were followed by the publication of poems in *New Directions 12* and the *Partisan Review* in the early 1950s. Seven poems also appeared in *Between Worlds* in the early 1960s.

The war may have inspired her return to poetry. The unpublished "America   A Miracle" is unabashedly patriotic, carrying the notation "Written when America entered World War II." The poem praises American greatness and confidently predicts that America will defeat the "man-of-prey," the "mechanised mon-

---

34. Mina Loy, "Insel" (Typescript in Collection of American Literature, Beinecke Rare Book and Manuscript Library, Yale University).
35. Julien Levy to the author, July 6, 1971.

ster" arisen in Europe. But as was the case with her initial reaction to World War I, Mina Loy seems most interested in the heightened perception she supposes nearness to death gives the soldier. In a letter to Van Vechten during World War I she wrote, "I've learnt how to be happy enough to live—and before I'm old enough for death—which doesn't happen to everyone!—I'm a little envious of these young men's eyes—going to the front!" And this unrelenting preoccupation with vision is a principal concern of "America   A Miracle": America's power is "an outcome of vision, / of keeping a pact with Deity / made in Lincolnian love of this nation." In "Aviator's Eyes," also from the early 1940s, American pilots represent the same nearness to final answers that Loy attributed to the soldiers of World War I: "Aviator's eyes / have indrawn the horizon / of drifting heaven." This continuing struggle for clear vision dominates the spiritual autobiography contained in Loy's poetry.

Another element of this reawakened interest in poetry may have been renewed contact with fellow artists, especially the Surrealists, the artistic expatriates of World War II. She had been friends with many of them in Europe, and in New York she was especially close to Peggy Guggenheim, Max Ernst, Joseph Cornell, and art dealer Colette Roberts. The Surrealist magazine *View* included her response to its 1942 questionnaire "Towards the Unknown" and reprinted "O Marcel . . . ," the montage of avant garde social life that had originally appeared in the *Blind Man*. This republication indicates how well Loy's genius spanned Dada and Surrealism, two of the most revolutionary art movements of the twentieth century.

The last and perhaps most important element of Mina Loy's return to poetry was the influence of New York City itself. Throughout her life she had been fascinated by human failure, and her poems of the 1940s are dominated by analyses of the examples she found in the streets and public places of the metropolis. Her move into the heart of the Bowery, alone, in 1951 seems the culmination of this interest. The long poem "Hot Cross Bum" (1949/1950) preceded this move, but out of the three-year Bowery residence came the paintings that comprised her 1959 show, "Constructions," at the Bodley Gallery in New York. A reviewer said that these paintings "reinvent the dead life of her derelict neighbors in terms of heaven and hell":

> *Bums Sleeping*, curled figures of stiffened folds of cloth, with arms clasped between their legs as though fettered, with painted, flat paper faces appealing directly upward (directly at *you*), plead to be released from the squared gray cement. In another invention, banana peels become licking flames around a trash can, out of which rises a butterfly whose wings are a flattened, pleated paper cup and whose body the spiral around a used vacuum-can key. That image, the plea of discarded life to be reanimated, inspires all of these works, in which the common becomes triumphant through a spiritual effort.[36]

The Bodley exhibit earned Loy the Copley Foundation Award for her painting, and gradually her poetry received belated attention.[37] A few literary historians, anthologists, and critics began in the early 1960s to follow Kenneth Rexroth's effort, "Les Lauriers Sont Coupés" (1944), to reintroduce Mina Loy as a seminal *American* modernist who provides instruction to contemporary poets. Rexroth admonished, "Mr. Laughlin, the 'Five Young Poets' are still Eliot, Stevens, Williams, Moore, Loy—get busy."[38] Fourteen years later Rexroth found a response in Jonathan Williams who published *Lunar Baedeker & Time-Tables* (1958), a collection of Mina Loy's poems. The attention of Williams and Rexroth is significant because they are postmodern poets, and it is as a precursor of postmodernism that Loy's place in the modernist vortex becomes clear. She belongs in the Stein–Pound–Williams–Moore current of modernism, the current that by generating postmodern poetry became the most vital force in Ameri-

36. A[nita] V[entura], "Mina Loy," *Arts*, XXXIII (April, 1959), 58.
37. "People in the Arts," *Arts*, XXXIV (February, 1960), 12.
38. Kenneth Rexroth, "Les Lauriers Sont Coupés," *Circle*, I, No. 4 (1944), 72.

can poetry. The other element of her contemporaneity is her highly individualistic feminism. However, Loy remains a largely unknown poet, undermined by early public indifference and confusion as well as her own lack of discipline and the attitude that, for her, poetry was only an avocation.

When Mina Loy left the Bowery in 1954, she joined her daughters Joella (Mrs. Herbert Bayer) and Fabi (Mrs. Fredric Benedict) in Aspen, Colorado. She continued to write and to paint but generally lost contact with the art world which had been a significant part of her life. After a short illness she died in Aspen on September 29, 1966.

CHAPTER ONE

The Female Self

The velocity of velocities arrives in starting.
    —"Aphorisms on Futurism" (1914)

Our person is a covered entrance to infinity
Choked with the tatters of tradition
    —"O Hell" (1920) [1]

Mina Loy, like the Futurists and many other moderns, may well have found in Walt Whitman the touchstone for her initial shrugging off of the "tatters of tradition." Whereas the Futurists admired Whitman's praise of progress, science, and technology, she would have been interested in his deification of the self, for her "a covered entrance to infinity." [2] In most of her early poetry she analyzes the female self as she sees its universal situation mirrored in her own life and the lives of her contemporaries. Her tone, however, is more pessimistic than Whitman's for she finds the divine fulfillment of the self obstructed by the laws and purposes of the universe—incomprehensible to the self but nevertheless shaping and limiting its perception, by its own flight from freedom, and, in the case of women, by repressive sexual mores. The essential sexual dimension of selfhood, important also to Whitman, is conveyed in the epigraph from the poem "O Hell." Selfhood is obstructed by sexual incompleteness: the body (a significant aspect of "our person") is a means ("entrance") to orgasmic self-realization ("infinity"), but selfhood is repressed ("covered") by traditional sexual propriety. The sex-

1. The first line appears in the pamphlet *Psycho-Democracy* as "'Self' is the covered entrance to Infinity." The last line is revised for *Lunar Baedeker* to read "Choked with the dusts of a tradition."

2. Raffaele Carrieri, *Futurism*, trans. Leslie van Rensselaer White (Milan: Edizioni del Milione, 1963), 8, 9, 26, 47, 147, notes the influence of Whitman on French art in the late nineteenth century and on Marinetti and the Futurists.

ual ecstasy of self-realization is more vividly imaged in the sky-rocket of the *Love Songs*: "I would   an   eye in a Bengal light / Eternity in a sky-rocket / Constellations in an ocean." Defending the sexual honesty of such poetry and of the magazines like *Others* and *Rogue* that printed it, Loy invokes, in a letter to Van Vechten (July, 1915), the example of Whitman and allies herself with the American literary revolt: "I believe we'll get more 'wholesome sex' in American art—than English after all—though you *are* considered so suburban—but that is to be expected—we haven't had a Whitman." She seems not to have written of Whitman again, but her poems on female selfhood answer his call for a poetry truthful to male and female sexuality:

> By silence or obedience the pens of savans, poets, historians, biographers, and the rest, have long connived at the filthy law, and books enslaved to it, that what makes the manhood of a man, that sex, womanhood, maternity, desires, lusty animations, organs, acts, are unmentionable and to be ashamed of, to be driven to skulk out of literature with whatever belongs to them. This filthy law has to be repealed—it stands in the way of great reforms. Of women just as much as men, it is the interest that there should not be infidelism about sex, but perfect faith. . . . I say that the body of a man or woman, the main matter, is so far quite unexpressed in poems; but that the body is to be expressed, and sex is.[3]

Whitman's immediate influence on Mina Loy can only be conjectured, but the contemporary feminist debate was certainly a stimulant to her thinking about the poetic use of the female experience. She seems to have read Havelock Ellis and she expressed curiosity about Margaret Sanger, of whose "'preventive' progaganda" she wrote Mabel Dodge (*ca.* 1914), "'*That's*' all nothing and yet '*that's*' all it is—the *more* is spiritual effervescence." Yet Loy distinguished her own interest from these and other practical voices of feminism. She inquired of Mrs. Dodge,

3. Whitman to Emerson, 1856, in *Leaves of Grass*, ed. Sculley Bradley and Harold W. Blodgett (New York: Norton, 1973), 739.

"Do tell me what you are making of Feminism. . . . Have you any idea in what direction the sex must be shoved—psychological I mean—bread and butter bores me rather." She also wrote to Van Vechten (*ca.* 1915) that "what I feel now are feminine politics—but in a cosmic way that may not fit in anywhere." In another letter she told him that the need she perceived was for psychic liberation based on sexual honesty: "I am quite hard hit by one remark of yours I had already made to my-self—'something without a sex undercurrent—'being so horribly ignorant—I know nothing about anything but life—and that is generally reducible to sex! But soon I shall have written through all I think about it—and then I shall develop some other vision of things[.] Also I think the Anglo-Saxon covered up-ness goes hand in hand with a reduction of the spontaneous creative quality . . . all this modern movement—is keeping entirely on the surface—and gets no further psychologically."

Mina Loy's overview of female liberation is contained in an unpublished "Feminist Manifesto."[4] Here she distinguishes her position from the economic and political solutions of the feminists and then rejects the notion that women are equal to men or that they should desire equality. (Her letters indicate that, at the least, she saw men as more intellectual, physically braver, and better able to bear pain.) She admonishes women to "leave off looking to men to find out what you are *not*—seek within yourselves to find out what you *are*." Woman is a parasite, limited by the male-imposed code of virtue to being either mother or mistress. Her success in the marriage market (hence, in life) depends on virginity. The cost to her is incompleteness of self and "an inadequate apprehension of *Life*." The unmarried woman is denied every woman's right to maternity. As the first step toward healthy female selfhood Loy proposes the "*unconditional* surgical

4. Mina Loy, "Feminist Manifesto," November 15, *ca.* 1914 (MS in Mabel Dodge Papers, Collection of American Literature, Beinecke Rare Book and Manuscript Library, Yale University).

destruction of virginity throughout the female population at puber-
ty" (a "daring" proposal that, she tells Mrs. Dodge [*ca.* 1914],
"had been suggested by some other woman years ago—see
Havelock Ellis"). Having discarded the fictive value of virginity,
woman could develop a more complete personality, assume
greater self-responsibility, and replace her "desire for comfort-
able protection" with "an intelligent curiosity and courage in
meeting and resisting the pressure of life." At the same time the
intelligent woman would fulfill her "race-responsibility" by pro-
ducing children, each a product of psychic health, "in adequate
proportion to the unfit or degenerate members of her sex." (This
allusion to a superior race anticipates Loy's hope, expressed in
the pamphlet *Psycho-Democracy*, for human evolution to greater
physical and psychic health and a more benevolent coexistence.)
The new woman will not think like men or share their employ-
ments. Rather, through sexual freedom she will gain emotional
independence: "Woman for her happiness must retain her deceptive fragility of appearance, combined with indomitable will,
irreducible courage, and abundant health[,] the outcome of
sound nerves—Another great illusion that woman must use all
her introspective clear-sightedness and unbiased bravery to destroy—for the sake of her *self respect* [—] is the impurity of sex[.]
The realisation in defiance of superstition that there is *nothing
impure in sex*—except in the mental attitude to it—will constitute
an incalculable and wider social regeneration than it is possible
for our generation to imagine."

The "Feminist Manifesto" probably owes several debts to Futurism, a local voice in the feminist debate of the 1910s. The aggressive tone and shocking defiance of convention echo Futurist
manifestoes. Nevertheless, her rejection of sexual equality chal-
lenges the Futurists' program. They scorned women as the embodiment of the *amore* to which the Italian male sentimentally
devoted himself at the expense of the technological world that
the Futurists prized as Italy's hope for cultural and political re-

juvenation. Not totally unsympathetic to women, Marinetti stated that with proper education they could become equal to men, and he supported the suffragists because, he said, "the more rights and powers they win for woman, the more will she be deprived of *Amore*, and by so much will she cease to be a magnet for sentimental passion or lust." He equated woman in her traditional roles to an animal: "It is plain that if modern woman dreams of winning her political rights, it is because without knowing it she is intimately sure of being, as a mother, as a wife, and as a lover, a closed circle, purely animal and wholly without usefulness."[5]

In illustration of Marinetti's sexual categories, the narrator of Loy's "One O'Clock at Night" (1915) is torn between female animal dependency and the aggressive intellectuality of her male companions. She has slipped into blissful passivity while the masculine voices of, presumably, a Futurist debate swirl around her:

Beautiful half-hour of being a mere woman
The animal woman
Understanding nothing of man
But mastery   and the security of imparted physical heat
Indifferent to cerebral gymnastics
Or regarding them as the self-indulgent play of children
Or the thunder of alien gods
But you woke me up
Anyhow   who am I that I should criticize your theories of plastic
    velocity

The line "But you woke me up," weighted with the personal and artistic innuendos of Mina Loy's coming to self-consciousness through contact with the Futurists, introduces along with the last line the defensive irony that characterizes her response to male

5. F. T. Marinetti, "Against *Amore* and Parliamentarianism," from *War, the World's Only Hygiene*, in R. W. Flint (ed.), *Marinetti: Selected Writings*, trans. R. W. Flint and Arthur A. Coppotelli (New York: Farrar, Straus and Giroux, 1972), 73, 75.

claims of superiority. Irony is her reality; the "Manifesto" a pipe dream. Irony pervades "Sketch of a Man on a Platform" (1915) where male intellectuality takes the form of schoolboy posturing. Though unnamed, the man easily assumes the Futurist carica- ture. He is forceful, "pushing / THINGS / In the opposite direction / To that which they are lethargically willing to go." The female observer, however, mocks his power, seeing his genius "So much less in your brain / Than in your body." He is "Fundamen- tally unreliable" and only superficially molds people, for "You leave others their initial strength." The implied contrast is be- tween the imperious male and the attentive female who is sup- posed to watch and applaud. The biting accusation of ineffective- ness revenges the woman whose own existence is lessened by the hollowness of the man on whom she ought to be able to rely.

This disappointment and the feeling of incompleteness it brings are, with the theme of sexual repression, the subjects of most of Mina Loy's poems of female selfhood. While the Futur- ists and their ideas are usually of secondary importance, many of the poems can be read as responses to Futurist attitudes to- ward women. The characters of the poems are Italian and En- glish women and girls, oppressed by Latin (and Futurist) ma- chismo or Loy's own English middle-class Victorian heritage. Both cultures doom women to dependence on men and sexual repression, but Loy's critique implies cultural differences in re- gard to means of repression. Italian girls are physically guarded —locked up—against uncontracted assaults on their person- hood, whereas English girls are so thoroughly educated in their culture's sexual mores that they are allowed to wander at large, protected from sexual enjoyment by their own fears and preju- dices.

The Italian virgin is so specifically the subject of "Virgins Plus Curtains Minus Dots" (1914/1915) that Mina Loy insisted to Van Vechten (*ca.* 1915) on the subtitle "Latin Borghese." For these virgins, dreams of love—"a god / White   with soft wings"—replace genuine living because they lack the dowery ("dots") for marriage. Poverty and propriety restrain them behind locked doors and curtained windows from where they "look out" at life's heroes:

> See the men pass
> Their hats are not ours
> We   take a walk
> They are going somewhere
> And they   may look   everywhere
> Men's eyes   look into things
> Our eyes   look out

Underlying the poem's obvious social commentary is sexual imagery that leads to the avowedly "metaphysical" preoccupation of all Mina Loy's poetry. The house, a symbol of the human body and the feminine principle, is locked and curtained, signifying virginity. The hatted men can, of course, open and enter the house if they desire. They have freedom, choice, purpose, vitality and, most important, penetrating vision. Their eyes "look into" life, permitting them attainment of selfhood, of "infinity." The eyes of the virgins (the curtained windows of the house), however, "look out": an otherness awaiting someone's permission to live. The two sets of eyes introduce Loy's major theme— the necessity of vision for self-realization. The self exists within an indifferent cosmos whose center is the life-giving, reality-defining sun. Selfhood is realized through the unremitting exercise of vision, for Loy a quest for self-and-world knowledge guided by the intuition. Woman in her extreme deprivation, denied the vision of her own physical reality, is emblematic of the blindness, in one form or another, that afflicts most of humanity.

Female blindness and otherness are embodied in the glass-eyed dolls in a Paris shop window in the poem "Magasins du Louvre" (1915). Representing the otherness of women put together to meet the needs of men, the dolls, "composite babies with arms extended," fill the shop, "Hang from the ceiling /

Beckoning / Smiling / In a profound silence." They, like the virgins, are objects to be bought and sold. And again sexual experience and vision are equated. Their selfhood, concentrated in the eye, is defined by their sexuality (suggested by the genital imagery of "parted fringes"), but in their ignorant purity these dolls see "nothing":

> All the virgin eyes in the world are made of glass
> They alone have the effrontery to
> Stare through the human soul
> Seeing nothing
> Between parted fringes

Mina Loy contrasts the blindness of the dolls to the knowledge of real women who must offer themselves in the sexual marketplace. The first is a shopgirl annoyed by a male shopwalker who, presumably, will try to buy her with flattery, petty gifts, and persistence. Two passing cocottes, like the dolls, are undisguised items of trade:

> One cocotte wears a bowler hat and a sham camelia
> And one an iridescent boa
> For there are two of them
> Passing
> And the solicitous mouth of one is straight
> The other curved into a static smile
> They see the dolls
> And for a moment their eyes relax
> To a flicker of elements unconditionally primeval

For the cocottes sexual experience has yielded the covert gaze rather than the assertive vision of realized selfhood: their eyes "now averted / Seek each other's—surreptitiously / To know if the other has seen." The narrator observes these glances and "entangles" her own eyes "with the pattern of the carpet / As eyes are apt to be / In their shame / Having surprised a gesture / That is ultimately intimate." The narrator's embarrassed understanding acknowledges her sisterhood with these demirep dolls.

This sisterhood includes the respectably married women of two poems that appeared in *Others'* anthology for 1917. In both Mina Loy employs the symbols of house and door, the female body and its "entrance," to express her theme of unfulfilled female selfhood. "At the Door of the House" (1914) recounts the unhappiness of Italian matrons for whom marriage has brought disillusion and resort to the card teller:

> A thousand women's eyes
> Riveted to the unrealisable
> Scatter the wash-stand of the card-teller
> Defiled marble of Carrara
>   On which she spreads
> Color-picture maps of destiny
> In the corner
> Of an inconducive bed-room

The cards unravel a tale of family intrigue, disillusion with marriage, and the temptation to adultery. The tone, phrasing, and imagery of the poem foreshadow the Tarot passage in T. S. Eliot's *The Waste Land* (1922):

> "Here is the Man of the Heart
> Turning his shoulders to a lady
> Covered with tears about matrimony
>
> At the door of your house
> There is a letter about an affair
> And a bed   and a table
> And this ace of spades turned upside-down
> 'With respect'
> Means   that some man
> Has   well you know
> Intentions   little honorable"

The second marriage poem, "The Effectual Marriage," was praised by Eliot as "extremely good,"[6] and Ezra Pound, who in 1931 called it one of the poems of the last thirty years which by

---

6. T. S. Apteryx [Eliot], "Observations," *Egoist*, V (1918), 70.

virtue of its "individual character" remained in his memory, twice reprinted it.[7] In both instances the poem is retitled "Ineffectual Marriage" and cut to a fifth of its original length, suggesting that Loy like Eliot benefited by Pound's editorial scissors. The original version picks up the door motif of "At the Door of the House," passing through the door—symbol of social and economic security, the mind, and entrance to the female body—into the life of one of the sad-eyed Italian matrons for whom sex is a conventional "quotidien" matter: "The door was an absurd thing / Yet it was passable / They quotidienly passed through it / It was this shape." Beyond the door reside Gina and Miovanni (obvious inversions of "Mina" and "Giovanni"). The scholarly Miovanni practices a kindly indifference to Gina, assuming her contentment with the sexual attentions and household he provides. Gina submits and adores him but qualifies her adoration with the fear that, daring a glance at the light of Miovanni's mind, she might be blinded, "Or even / That she should see   Nothing at all." They have made their marital door "passable," but the ideal fails in Miovanni's haughty isolation and Gina's enslavement to love. Their marriage possesses only a negative completeness; each supports the other's self-deceptions and is thus aided in living a lie. Miovanni's dependence on Gina dominates the shortened version, first in abstract analysis and then in the striking image of the madonna with a man hidden beneath her crinoline:

> So here we might dispense with her
> Gina being a female
> But she was more than that
> Being an incipience   a correlative
> an instigation of the reaction of man
> From the palpable to the transcendent
> Mollescent irritant of his fantasy

7. Ezra Pound, *Profile: An Anthology Collected in 1931* (Milan: John Scheilwiller, 1932), 13, 67–68; Pound previously printed the poem in "In the Vortex," in *Instigations* (New York: Boni and Liveright, 1920), 240.

> Gina had her use   Being useful
> contentedly conscious
> She flowered in Empyrean
> From which no well-mated woman ever returns
>
> Sundays   a warm light in the parlor
> From the gritty road   on the white wall
> anybody could see it
> Shimmered a composite effigy
> Madonna   crinolined   a man
> hidden beneath her hoop

The longer poem moves to a final image of Gina in her kitchen among

> The scrubbed smell of the white-wood table
> Greasy cleanliness   of the chopper board
> The coloured vegetables
> Intuited quality of flour
> Crickly sparks of straw-fanned charcoal.

Place of Gina's seeming happiness, the kitchen—keeping with the house-body symbolism—appropriately is also the place of her "psychic transmutation,"[8] for the description of the kitchen is followed by an abrupt addendum which notes Gina's move from blindness to vision: "(This narrative halted when I learned that the house which inspired it was the home of a mad woman.)"

The English version of female repression appears in the long, semi-autobiographical *Anglo-Mongrels and the Rose*. With a nod to the thirteenth-century love allegory *Le Roman de la Rose*, *Anglo-Mongrels* employs the social satire of Jean de Meung to create a contemporary allegory of love. The poem relates the courtship and marriage of Exodus, a Hungarian-Jewish immigrant, and Alice, a middle-class, virginal English rose. She—filled with

> Maiden emotions
> bread

8. J. E. Cirlot, *A Dictionary of Symbols*, trans. Jack Sage (London: Routledge & Kegan Paul, 1962), 146.

> on leaves of novels
> where anatomical man
> has no notion
> of offering other than the bended knee
> to femininity

—is as ignorant and idealistic as her Italian counterparts. Allowed to ramble freely, in "belligerent innocence" among the "thick hedgerows / where she blows / on Christian Sundays," she meets and entices Exodus. And when he, successful in his marriage offer, "Oriental / mad to melt / with something softer than himself / clasps with soothing pledges / his wild rose of the hedges," she hysterically rejects him. His passion

> splinters upon an adamite
> opposition
> of nerves like stalactites
>
> This dying chastity
> had rendered up no soul———

The marriage becomes a hotbox of hostility where Alice and Exodus prey upon each other in bitter disillusion and unwittingly obstruct the psychic growth of their child Ova.

To the stunted lives of the women in these poems Mina Loy opposes a dream of human possibility shaped by her acquaintance with the ideas of Whitman, the Futurists, and French philosopher Henri Bergson. Her earliest assault against the restrictions upon the self, especially those derived from the past, is the "Aphorisms on Futurism," fifty-one prescriptions for self-liberation. She ignores Futurist devotion to technology except as speed and energy are useful images of a positive, aggressive confrontation of life. Each aphorism is informed by the faith that "the smallest person, potentially, is as great as the Universe." One must cut free from the darkness of the past. "The Future is only dark from outside. / *Leap* into it—and it EXPLODES with *Light*." Old self-and-world definitions must be abandoned: "There are no excrescences on the absolute, to which man may pin his faith"; "Forget that you live in houses, that you may live in yourself." One must throw off prejudices and psychic restraint, "the mechanical re-actions of the subconsciousness, that rubbish heap of race-tradition." "Joy," "Intuition," and "Inspiration" must replace "Misery," "Intellect," and "Acceptance." The individual has the power to shape self and world: "Not to be a cipher in your ambient, / But to color your ambient with your preferences." The "Aphorisms" are a call to awakening: "Today is the crisis in consciousness."

Few of Mina Loy's narrators or characters attain the self-fulfillment hailed by the "Aphorisms"; but several poems, drawing upon the Italian commoners she observed from her home in the Costa San Giorgio, capture the vitality that was for her the most important element of Futurism. The three-poem sequence "Italian Pictures" (1914) depicts Italians who lead energetic, spontaneous, and sometimes cruel lives. They live unreflectingly with their poverty, ignorance, and ancient culture, integrating their biological, spiritual, and emotional being. Self-conscious and isolated English characters and narrators are foils to the Italians. "July in Vallombrosa" presents an elderly English invalid, recuperating in Italy and attended by a daughter whose life is spent "In chasing moments from one room to another / When the essence of an hour / Was in its passing." Their misused lives, however, are not completely squandered, because the money for their upkeep "Goes to support / The loves / Of head-waiters." The narrator of "The Costa San Giorgio" similarly contrasts refinement and vitality: "We English make a tepid blot / On the messiness / Of the passionate Italian life-traffic / Throbbing the street." "Costa Magic," omitting the cultural comparison, relates a folk-tale incident about an unmarried girl whose father, "Indisposed to her marriage / And a rabid man at that," places a curse on her that leads to her death.

These Italians are commonplace deities similar to the deformed mythological figures in William Carlos Williams' *Kora in Hell*. Appropriately, "Summer Night in a Florentine Slum" (1920) appeared in Williams' and Robert McAlmon's *Contact* magazine. The English narrator, with a copy of Aubrey Beardsley's *Mlle De Maupin* (symbol of art-for-art's-sake rejection of life) on the wall, observes the indolent Italian life-traffic:

> The dust was hot, the dust was dry—it lay low, it travelled about; and among it, Latin families lay on the lousy stones, in what they could manage of an earthy abandon.
>
> They sprawled among each other, lightly ragged—heavy breathing —men, with their offspring flung into sleep across their pelvises— blowing the life out of their Toscani cigars—among their messy curls—and the lubricous eyes of their women waited on them from the darkness.

Such primitive abandon was not a viable alternative for a sophisticated English woman. And of course Mina Loy was attracted not by the specific Italian life-style but by the unity of self and environment that the Italians demonstrate. She seems to have found something of a personal solution in the metaphysics of Henri Bergson. His ideas pervaded early twentieth-century thought and may have come to Mina Loy directly or through the Futurists.[9] According to Bergson the self, complementing intellect with intuition, seeks its inner essence and oneness with cosmic becoming. Through an intuitive plunge into innermost being, the self discovers its existence to be a perpetual becoming—a duration (*durée*)—in which it is shaped by the past but enabled through the risk of action to spontaneously create itself in new directions. Existence, says Bergson, is endless self-creation.[10]

Mina Loy confirms her familiarity with Bergson's ideas in an appreciative explanation of Gertrude Stein's writing. Referring to Stein's "Galeries Lafayette" (1911/1915), she says: "This was when Bergson was in the air, and his beads of Time strung on the continuous flux of Being, seemed to have found a literary

9. Carrieri, *Futurism*, 80.
10. Henri Bergson, *Creative Evolution*, trans. Arthur Mitchell (New York: Modern Library, 1944), 7–10.

conclusion in the austere verity of Gertrude Stein's theme—
'Being' as the absolute occupation." Bergson's influence differs
in the writings of Stein and Loy, although both were interested
in the act of consciousness. Stein violated traditional syntax and
employed repetition to record the subtle alterations, from moment to moment, in the object observed and the consciousness
observing it. Loy describes the result:

> By the intervaried rhythm of this monotone mechanism she uses for
> inducing a continuity of awareness of her subject, I was connected up
> with the very pulse of duration.
>
> The core of a "Being" was revealed to me with uninterrupted insis-
> tence.
>
> The plastic static of the ultimate presence of an entity.[11]

Consciousness as it emerges from Loy's poetic inquiries into
how one knows and what it is possible to know is a dynamic
alternation of abstract, analytical passages and vivid concrete
images. The alternation represents fluctuations of the self between states of intellectual and intuitive being. Her concern is
not the unchanging nature of one's manner of experiencing the
world, but the possibilities for experience, for becoming. Bergson's *Creative Evolution* (1907), source of the "beads of Time,"
supplies the form and much of the substance of her inquiry.

Especially in "Parturition" (1914) is Bergson's presence felt.
The poem is significant among Loy's explorations of female selfhood because it details an area of femaleness rarely thought
suitable for literature, and because it unites the spiritual and intellectual life with the physical. She has tried to free woman
from passive slavery to her unique pain by using pain creatively
to arrive at a clear understanding of the female experience.[12] In
giving birth to the child, she gives birth to her self:

11. Mina Loy, "Gertrude Stein," *Transatlantic Review*, II (1924), 305–306.
12. See Adrienne Rich, *Of Woman Born: Motherhood as Experience and Institu-
tion* (New York: Norton, 1976), 158. Citing Simone Weil, Rich distinguishes between pain as creative work and passive slavery.

I am the centre
Of a circle of pain
Exceeding its boundaries in every direction

The business of the bland sun
Has no affair with me
In my congested cosmos of agony
From which there is no escape
On infinitely prolonged nerve-vibrations
Or in contraction
To the pin-point nucleus of being

Locate an irritation   without
It is   within
          within
It is without
The sensitized area
Is identical   with the extensity
Of intension

I am the false quantity
In the harmony of physiological potentiality
To which
Gaining self-control
I should be consonant
In time

Pain is no stronger than the resisting force
Pain calls up in me
The struggle is equal

The open window is full of a voice
A fashionable portrait-painter
Running up-stairs to a woman's apartment
Sings
          "All the girls are tid'ly did'ly
          All the girls are nice
          Whether they wear their hair in curls
          Or—"
At the back of the thoughts to which I permit crystallization
The conception   Brute
Why?
          The irresponsibility of the male

Leaves woman her superior Inferiority
He is running up-stairs

I am climbing a distorted mountain of agony
Incidentally with the exhaustion of control
I reach the summit
And gradually subside into anticipation of
Repose
Which never comes
For another mountain is growing up
Which   goaded by the unavoidable
I must traverse
Traversing myself

Something in the delirium of night-hours
Confuses while intensifying sensibility
Blurring spatial contours
So aiding elusion of the circumscribed
That the gurgling of a crucified wild beast
Comes from so far away
And the foam on the stretched muscles of a mouth
Is no part of myself
There is a climax in sensibility
When pain surpassing itself
Becomes exotic
And the ego succeeds in unifying the positive and negative
      poles of sensation
Uniting the opposing and resisting forces
In lascivious revelation

Relaxation
Negation of myself as a unit
      Vacuum interlude
I should have been emptied of life
Giving life
For consciousness in crises   races
Through the subliminal deposits of evolutionary processes
Have I not
Somewhere
Scrutinized
A dead white feathered moth
Laying eggs?

A moment
Being realization
Can
Vitalized by cosmic initiation
Furnish an adequate apology
For the objective
Agglomeration of activities
Of a life
LIFE
A leap with nature
Into the essence
Of unpredicted maternity
Against my thigh
Touch of infinitesimal motion
Scarcely perceptible
Undulation
Warmth   moisture
Stir of incipient life
Precipitating into me
The contents of the universe
Mother I am
Identical
With infinite Maternity
    Indivisible
    Acutely
    I am absorbed
    Into
The was—is—ever—shall—be
Of cosmic reproductivity

Rises from the subconscious
Impression of a cat
With blind kittens
Among her legs
Same undulating life—stir
I am that cat

Rises from the subconscious
Impression of small animal carcass
Covered with blue-bottles
—Epicurean—
And through the insects

Waves that same undulation of living
Death
Life
I am knowing
All about
    Unfolding

The next morning
Each woman-of-the-people
Tip-toeing the red pile of the carpet
Doing hushed service
Each woman-of-the-people
Wearing a halo
A ludicrous little halo
Of which she is sublimely   unaware

I once heard in a church
—Man and woman God made them—
                Thank God.

The opening declaration "I am" reappears six times to assert
the goal of self-definition. Childbirth provides the Bergsonian
moment necessary for self-comprehension: "Let us seek, in the
depths of our experience, the point where we feel ourselves
most intimately within our own life. It is into pure duration that
we then plunge back, a duration in which the past, always moving on, is swelling unceasingly with a present that is absolutely
new." [13] That childbirth provides *the* moment when the speaker is
"most intimately within" her life points again to Mina Loy's belief
in the inescapable difference in the sexes. Woman needs psychological freedom but biology determines that her freedom will be
unique.

The first twenty-three lines re-create the space of the speaker's existence. Her anguished personal cosmos lies within a natural cosmos other than and indifferent to her suffering. To understand her relation to the universe she must, according to

13. Bergson, *Creative Evolution*, 218–19.

Bergson, merge the personal cosmos with the natural one. The former is pictured as a circle containing an essential "centre," or a "nucleus of being" which is the object of discovery. This circle, says Bergson, is the "circle of the given" which our reason defines for us but which can be broken by thrusting reason aside and risking action in a new direction.[14] The circle also recalls Marinetti's characterization of woman in her traditional roles as a closed circle (in contrast to the straight line and terminal, Futurist symbols of masculine purpose and action). For the I of "Parturition" childbirth provides the action, the means of breaking through the boundaries of the self. The woman begins to "exceed" her boundaries but remains separated from the natural cosmos with which she desires to identify herself: "The business of the bland sun / Has no affair with me"; "I am the false quantity / In the harmony of physiological potentiality." Her own being, however, is unified. The "within" and "without"—the "nucleus of being" and all external to it—merge in their shared, inescapable torment. *Extension* and *intension* are Bergson's terms. Extension—the intellectual arrangement of the parts of the whole as external to each other—is the spatialization of pain in the physical body; intension—the instinctual knowledge of the wholeness of the object—is the integration of her being in time.[15]

Throughout the poem, irregular line length and internal spacing reflect the spasms of pain and the metaphysical quest shaped by them. Passages of abstract analysis are interspersed with concrete images to indicate the I's oscillation between intellect and intuition.

The first image captures the separateness of male and female experience. The portrait painter is off to a sexual encounter, leaving another exploited woman to pay for an adventure he has already forgotten. It is he, the "Brute," Mina Loy seems to an-

14. *Ibid.*, 211.
15. *Ibid.*, 169–70, 164–65.

swer Marinetti, who is the animal. The male's careless sexual freedom—"He is running up-stairs"—contrasts sharply to the female's tormented physical and spiritual climbing of a "mountain of agony," a climbing by which she finally achieves identification of self and natural cosmos in an orgasmic "lascivious revelation." (The "covered entrance," the vaginal door, becomes the means in childbirth by which woman knows "infinity.") But considerable irony pervades the revelation. For as "spatial contours" blur, "So aiding elusion of the circumscribed," the speaker intuits that the duration she shares with the natural cosmos is only indifferent evolutionary process. Her cries echo those of the "gurgling of a crucified wild beast"; the images of being that follow confirm this animal aspect of her "infinite Maternity." She is the "dead white feathered moth / Laying eggs," the cat "With blind kittens / Among her legs"; she is part of the life and death flux imaged in the "small animal carcass / Covered with blue-bottles." Having plunged into her deepest self to discover her oneness with universal becoming, the I perceives herself as an insignificant molecule within "evolutionary processes."

The final image of female solicitude and the sisterhood of suffering (counterpart of the image of male exploitation) offers human affection within this brutal life struggle. However, the "ludicrous little halo" implies the relative unimportance of these efforts. The addendum, omitted when the poem was reprinted in 1923, seems ironic. To thank God, whose traditional definition the poem has nullified, for this vision of the animality by which woman is martyred for the survival of the race is blasphemy.

Thus, using a metaphysics which could be expected to lead to an intuition of freedom and possibility, Mina Loy rediscovers woman's limitation and helplessness, and also woman's strength. She has proven Marinetti's accusation of female animality, but she has also defied animality by using suffering creatively. The disillusion of this necessary human compromise with the ideal, protectively masked in characteristic irony, is at the heart of her quest for selfhood. The quest begins with her rebellion against restrictions on female selfhood and continues in the *Love Songs* (discussed later) to discovery of the difficulty of adapting to freedom when one's emotions are educated to the need for romantic love.

The poems of the female self are an important preparation for Mina Loy's later work. They construct the metaphysics that shapes all her poetry and ground the spiritual autobiography in uniquely female experience. Sometimes inferior in line, word, and image to later poems, they introduce the technical and structural experiment that is one of Loy's major contributions to American modernism. And they are a distinctive statement in the feminist debate, filling in their metaphysics with a tough-eyed analysis of woman's sexual-psychological and, to a lesser extent, socioeconomic oppression. Few, if any, of the other female poets of the era speak so honestly about the quotidian life of woman. Compared to confessional poetry or today's feminist poetry, Mina Loy's poems, with the exception of "Parturition" and the *Love Songs*, may not seem daring. But Mina Loy felt the conflict between social respectability and the poetic honesty crucial to her own well-being. Writing to Van Vechten (*ca.* summer, 1915) of her need to use sexuality in her work, she says, "You know I am quite glad of all I write but occasionally get scared of my family—but I am going to just risk everything—and not bother." Similarly, in the spring of 1916 rumor reached her that her meandering husband, halted temporarily in New York, was suggesting that her work was "offensive" and she fit to associate only with "outcasts." She asks Van Vechten, "Now my dear I've got a beautiful daughter—I cant *outcast*—what shall I do[?] reassure me—I have tried my things on *ultra respectable* elderly ladies (not stupid ones of course) and they survive magnificently—will America be so *very* different?" The limited American public for the new poetry seems to have been less sympathetic than the wise ladies of the old world, but whether or not concern for respectability curtailed Mina Loy's analysis of female selfhood is a moot question. I suspect new interests, not fear of the public's disapproval, lessened the number of her poems on women. Nevertheless, her comments reflect the risks she felt she took as a woman and a poet in treating the female experience.

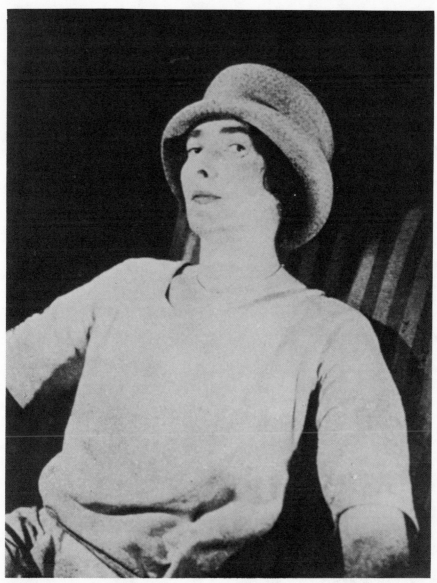

Mina Loy. Photograph in the *Little Review*, Vol. VIII
(September–December, 1920).

Mina Loy and Djuna Barnes. Nice, France. Photograph by
Natalie Barney. Courtesy of Mrs. Herbert Bayer and Mrs. Fredric Benedict

Mina Loy. Photograph for naturalization papers. New York. April 15, 1946. Courtesy of Mrs. Herbert Bayer and Mrs. Fredric Benedict

Mina Loy. Photograph by Jonathan Williams. Aspen,
Colorado, 1957. Courtesy of Mrs. Herbert Bayer and Mrs. Fredric Benedict

Arthur Cravan. Photograph in *The Soil*, No. 4 (April, 1917).

Courtesy of the Beinecke Rare Book and Manuscript Library, Yale University

Love Songs.

I.

Spawn of Fantasies
Silting the appraisable
Pig Cupid   his rosy snout
Rooting erotic garbage
"Once upon a time"
Pulls a weed   white star-topped
Among wild oats sown in mucous-membrane
I would   an eye in a Bengal light
Eternity in a sky-rocket
Constellations in an Ocean
Whose rivers run no fresher
Than a trickle of saliver

~~These are~~

These are suspect places

I must live in my lantern
Trimming subliminal flicker
Virginal   to the bellows
Of Experience

Coloured glass

Mina Loy.
1915.

Poem I of the *Love Songs*.

L'Amour Dorloté par les Belles Dames (ca. 1912).

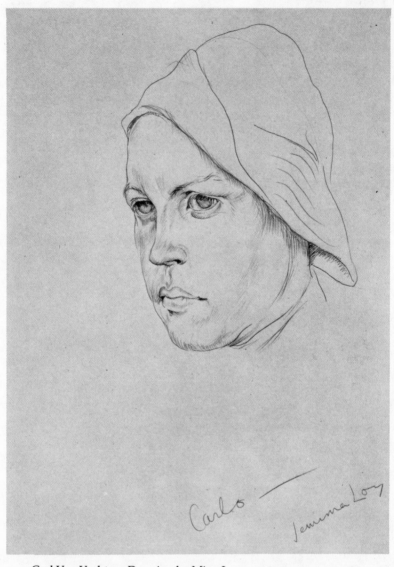

Carl Van Vechten. Drawing by Mina Loy.
Courtesy of the Beinecke Rare Book and Manuscript Library, Yale University

CHAPTER TWO
The Modernist Vision

I *Futurism*   The Futurist can live a thousand years
in one poem.

He can compress every aesthetic principle in one line.

—"Aphorisms on Futurism"

The notoriety of Mina Loy's poetry was due only in part to its honest analysis of female experience. Her poems were also first-hand assimilations of current structural and technical experiments by European painters and writers, especially the Futurists. As such they defied American expectations of how a poem should mean and look. Alfred Kreymborg, poet and enthusiastic supporter of modern poets, explains the reaction to Mina Loy's poems in *Others*: "Detractors shuddered at Mina Loy's subject-matter and derided her elimination of punctuation marks and the audacious spacing of her lines. These technical factors not only crop up in a later poet, E. E. Cummings, to whose originality later critics have attributed them, but were learned by Mina during a lengthy sojourn in Paris and Florence, where she came under the influence of Guillaume Apollinaire and F. T. Marinetti. Mina had simply transferred futuristic theories to America, and in her subject-matter had gone about expressing herself freely —another continental influence." Even an eager modern like Kreymborg sometimes found Mina Loy difficult. He recalls that "no manuscripts required more readings than those of Mina Loy and Marianne Moore." [1]

There are no extant manuscripts to indicate what kind of poetry, if any, Mina Loy wrote before she came under Futurist influ-

1. Alfred Kreymborg, *Troubadour: An Autobiography* (New York: Boni and Liveright, 1925), 235–36, 242.

ence. Later poems suggest that in poetry as in painting her immediate heritage was the Decadence. The rhymed, basically iambic lines of the unpublished poem "The Beneficent Garland" (January, 1914) indicate that her earliest poetry was structurally traditional and prosaic:

> To hang about the knees of the gods,
> The first-fruits of the awful odds
> 'Gainst which man till'd the soil.
>
> *   *   *   *   *   *
>
> What are these these first fruits, I pray
> Swelling at night, to ripen by day
> Such sorrows of their toil?
>
> *   *   *   *   *   *
>
> Fruits of this mystery are they born
> The baby and the ear of corn,
> Hunger and drawing breath.[2]

If it is difficult to locate Loy's poetic beginnings, it is relatively easy to determine the crucial contributions of Futurism to her poetry around 1913–1914. In addition to the psychic stimulation the Futurists offered the emerging poet and her beleaguered female self, Futurist paintings, poems, and technical manifestoes suggested alternative poetic structures. Because little is known of Mina Loy's life from 1907–1912, it is impossible to assert that her conversion was sudden, although her testimony to the general influence of Futurism on her life indicates a fairly abrupt awakening. By 1913 she did know the Futurists and must have been reading *Lacerba*, a bimonthly review published in Florence by Ardengo Soffici and Giovanni Papini. Introduced on January 1, 1913, *Lacerba* published the Futurists as well as French writers such as Remy de Gourmont, Apollinaire, and Max Jacob; and it

2. Mina Loy, "The Beneficent Garland" (MS in Mabel Dodge Papers, Collection of American Literature, Beinecke Rare Book and Manuscript Library, Yale University).

printed sketches by leading modernist painters.[3] Mina Loy may also have been receiving the magazines of the French avant garde, as she was later to receive American publications like *Trend* and *Rogue*. The apparent rapidity with which she assimilated the new techniques was due probably to the convergence of personal and artistic needs with radical solutions and to the sensibility of both painter and poet which aided her adaptation of the innovations of one medium to the other.

A deceptively simple instance of Loy's use of Futurist theory is "The Costa San Giorgio" (1914). The poem's re-creation of Italian street life, the sort of subject that appealed to Futurist painters, requires no understanding of Futurism. Its vignettes, in spite of experimental typography and the absence of punctuation, are structured by conventional syntax. Thematically the poem contrasts the vitality of the street to the fixity of the English, the church, an invalid, and the Italian home:

> We English make a tepid blot
> On the messiness
> Of the passionate Italian life-traffic
> Throbbing the street   up   steep
> Up   up   to the porta
> Culminating
> In the stained fresco of the dragon-slayer
>
> The hips of women sway
> Among the crawling children they produce
> And the church hits the barracks
> Where
> The greyness of marching men
> Falls through the greyness of stone
>
> Oranges half-rotten are sold at a reduction
> Hoarsely advertised as broken heads
> BROKEN HEADS   and the barber

3. Raffaele Carrieri, *Futurism*, trans. Leslie van Rensselaer White (Milan: Edizioni del Milione, 1963), 106.

Has an imitation mirror
And Mary preserve our mistresses from seeing us as we see ourselves
Shaving
ICE CREAM
Licking is larger than mouths
Boots than feet
Slip   slap   and the string dragging
And the angle of the sun
Cuts the whole lot in half

And warms the folded hands
Of a consumptive
Left outside   her chair is broken
And she wonders how we feel
For we walk very quickly
The noonday cannon
Having scattered the neighbour's pigeons

The smell of small cooking
From luckier houses
Is cruel to the maimed cat
Hiding
Among carpenter's shavings
From three boys
—One holding a bar—
Who nevertheless
Born of human parents
Cry when locked in the dark

Fluidic blots of sky
Shift among roofs
Between bandy legs
Jerk patches of street
Interrupted by clacking
Of all the green shutters
From which
Bits of bodies
Variously leaning
Mingle eyes with the commotion

For there is little to do
The false pillow-spreads

Hugely initialed
Already adjusted
On matrimonial beds
And the glint on the china virgin
Consummately dusted

Having been thrown
Anything or something
That might have contaminated intimacy
OUT
Onto the middle of the street

The heading "Italian Pictures" under which "The Costa San Giorgio" is grouped, with "July in Vallombrosa" and "Costa Magic," hints at the poem's painterly aspirations.[4] Keeping with the artistic temper of the time, however, Loy's goal is not the superficially realistic reproduction of one scene at one moment, but the creation of the vibrant movement of the street and thereby of the energy of life. She has adopted the Futurist imperative: "THAT UNIVERSAL DYNAMISM MUST BE RENDERED AS DYNAMIC SENSATION."[5]

To structure "The Costa San Giorgio" as a dynamic canvas, rather than as a narrative or realistic painting, Loy employs techniques of the Futurist and Cubist painters to destroy the illusion of three-dimensional space. Overlapping planes, juxtapositions, signs, and fractured images stress the two-dimensional flat space of her poem-canvas. The transformation from narrative to Futurist canvas begins in the first line. Linear development yields to a depthless pictorial surface as the speaker and her English fellows become a "tepid blot" on the messy Italian landscape, an abstract element of form, color, and motion compositionally related to the "Fluidic blots of sky," "green shutters," and "Bits of bodies."

4. "July in Vallombrosa" and "Costa Magic" employ the typographical irregularities and colloquial tone of "The Costa San Giorgio," but their structure and imagery do not make the latter's allusions to the techniques of painting.
5. *Technical Manifesto of Futurist Painting* (1910), quoted in Carrieri, *Futurism*, 32.

Blots of paint signifying the sky destroy the illusion of atmospheric depth. Likewise, the sun at the end of stanza three is reduced to a geometric form, a sign that stands for sunlight. In stanza two Cézanne's technique of *passage*, "the running together of planes otherwise separated in space," [6] is employed in "falls through" to make one dimension of the greyness of war, men, church, and stones—the extensions and opposites of the lively women and children. In stanza six the verbs "shift" and "jerk" energize the atmosphere into moving shapes on the canvas. Pictorial realism is also distorted by the exaggeration of visual, auditory, and kinetic fragments so that they dominate the wholes to which they belong. "BROKEN HEADS," "ICE CREAM," and "OUT" balloon above the poem; and "shutters," "Bits of bodies," and "eyes" dominate the buildings and bodies to which they belong.

As the speaker recedes to a minor compositional element in the opening line, she and the reader merge with the chaotic vitality of the street, losing much of their interpretative distance: objectivity is supplanted by consciousness-in-the-world. The Futurists included this shift of perspective in their technical manifesto of painting: "Painters have always shown persons and objects as if arranged in front of us. We shall place the spectator in the centre of the painting." [7]

Mina Loy's chief pictorial means for creating the flux of life, as well as two-dimensional space, is collage, a structure used by the Futurists and derived perhaps from Analytical Cubism. Collage brings together, as though simultaneously present, the diverse physical and psychological perspectives on a scene or object. That is, it juxtaposes without logical connections diverse fragments of experience in order to create the dynamic complexity of life. The Futurists juxtapose the multiple dimensions and movements of an object as well as the environment in which the object exists and the feelings of those who observe and partici-

6. Edward F. Fry (ed.), *Cubism* (New York: McGraw-Hill, n.d.), 14.
7. Carrieri, *Futurism*, 32.

pate in a scene. Futurist painter and sculptor Umberto Boccioni, in quoting the preface to the first Paris exhibit of Futurist painting (1912), explains the aim:

> "The simultaneity of states of mind in the work of art: that is the exhilarating aim of our art. . . . When painting a person on a balcony seen from the interior, we do not limit the scene to that which the frame of the window permits us to see; we force ourselves to present the entire series of plastic sensations felt by the painter whilst standing on the balcony: the sun-drenched crowds in the street; the double row of houses which extends to both right and left; other balconies with flowering plants, etc. All of which signifies simultaneity of environment and, therefore, the dislocation and dismemberment of objects and the scattering fusion of details are individually independent. In order to make the spectator live in the centre of the painting . . . it is necessary that the painting be a synthesis of that which one remembers and that which one sees. It is necessary to render the invisible that stirs and lives beyond the walls—that which we have on our left and on our right and behind us—and not just the little scene of artificial life framed as if between curtains of a Stage."[8]

In poetry Apollinaire, friend of the Futurists and one of the first simultaneists, achieves the same complexity in *Zone* (1912). Walking through the Paris streets, the thirty-three-year-old poet reviews his life in discontinuous images, fantastic and realistic, of past and present. Juxtaposed without transitions, these images make varieties of experience simultaneously present.[9] Mina Loy's evocation of the Costa San Giorgio is less disjunctive than *Zone* because her images are homogeneous and realistic. She utilizes activities occurring along one street within a few minutes rather than scenes from a life. However, like Apollinaire she minimizes transitions between images, relying instead on the mind's associations.

The basic units of juxtaposition in "The Costa San Giorgio" are the stanzas that divide the street into "its inherent tenden-

8. *Ibid.*, 123.
9. Marcel Raymond, *From Baudelaire to Surrealism* (London: Peter Owen, 1961), 234.

cies of movement and form." Scenes of activity abut stationary scenes, just as a Futurist painting might juxtapose a sphere and cone to "give the impression of a dynamic force beside a static force."[10] Stanza three, for example, explodes with movement and sound: the selling of oranges, shaving, eating "ICE CREAM," and the slip-slapping of shoes. In contrast the opening of stanza four presents an immobile invalid whose sole activity is mental: she "wonders." Joining the two stanzas, "the angle of the sun / Cuts the whole lot in half // And warms the folded hands / Of a consumptive." The angular sunray, a familiar element in Mina Loy's poetic universe and a frequent sign for atmospheric light on Futurist canvases, provides dynamic thrust.

Dynamism does not cease with the tension between stanzas. Within each stanza Loy creates the inner movement of the scene through typography, colloquial speech, verbs, and small-scale juxtapositions. In addition to Futurist painting, Marinetti's literary theories seem influential in her creation of motion. In the *Technical Manifesto of Futurist Literature* (1912) he advocates radical departures from conventional literary form and image:

1. One must destroy syntax and scatter one's nouns at random, just as they are born.
2. One should use infinitives, because they adapt themselves elastically to nouns and don't subordinate them to the writer's *I* that observes or imagines. . . .
3. One must abolish the adjective, to allow the naked noun to preserve its essential color. . . .
4. One must abolish the adverb, old belt buckle that holds two words together. . . .
5. Every noun should have its double; that is, the noun should be followed, with no conjunction, by the noun to which it is related by analogy. Example: man-torpedo-boat, woman-gulf, crowd-surf, piazza-funnel, door-faucet. . . .

10. See Werner Haftmann, *Painting in the Twentieth Century: An Analysis of the Artists and Their Work*, trans. Ralph Manheim (2 vols.; New York: Frederick A. Praeger, 1965), I, 108. Haftmann calls this external movement *"absolute movement"* and the "actual motion" of an object *"relative movement."*

6. Abolish even the punctuation. . . .

7. [Images] are the very lifeblood of poetry. Poetry should be an uninterrupted sequence of new images, or it is mere anemia and greensickness. . . .

8. There are no categories of images, noble or gross or vulgar, eccentric or natural. The intuition that grasps them has no preferences or *partis pris*. . . .

9. To render the successive motions of an object, one must render the *chain of analogies* that it evokes, each condensed and concentrated into one essential word. . . .

10. Destroy the *I* in literature: that is, all psychology. . . . Be careful not to force human feelings onto matter. . . .[11]

These prescriptions inform much of Mina Loy's poetry, although she finds some, like the rejection of adjectives and adverbs and the elimination of the I, uncongenial to her metaphysics. In "The Costa San Giorgio" she abolishes punctuation and uses an innovative typography that includes "Pauses of the intuition" and "SMALL CAPITALS for violent onomatopoeia."[12] Typography and free verse convey the street rhythms, just as in "Parturition" they echo the mental and physical rhythms of a woman in labor. Colloquial phrasing and typography combine to evoke the inner worlds of the street people. Loy ignores Marinetti's injunction to rely on the infinitive, but she does exhibit extreme verb consciousness. Numerous present participles, gerunds, and present-tense verbs create continuous movement; and surely "anything" and "something"—the troublesome vitality that has been tossed into the street—are selected for their resemblance to the participle. Verbs and verb forms are positioned for emphasis, and the juxtaposition of movement and stasis continues in the contrast of present-tense verbs and participles to past participles. The latter depict the finished, the hopeless, the nonvital aspects of the scene: the fresco is "stained"; the

11. R. W. Flint (ed.), *Marinetti: Selected Writings*, trans. R. W. Flint and Arthur A. Coppotelli (New York: Farrar, Straus and Giroux, 1972), 84–87.

12. F. T. Marinetti, "Wireless Imagination and Words at Liberty," trans. Arundel del Re, *Poetry and Drama*, III (1913), 323, 325.

consumptive sits with "folded" hands (she has been "left" in a "broken" chair, like the "maimed" cat she is defenseless); the boys cry when "locked" in the dark; and inside quiet homes pillow spreads are "initialed" and "adjusted," the china virgin "dusted."

In the creation of external and internal movement Marinetti's theory of the image is important in "The Costa San Giorgio." His claim that poetry should be "an uninterrupted sequence of new images" governs the structure of the poem, and within several stanzas juxtaposed images reflect the movement of the eye and make visual puns. In stanza three, for example, syntax lapses as the eye jumps from the "BROKEN HEADS" of the orange vendor to the heads shaved by the barber, and the shaving cream of the latter becomes "ICE CREAM." (The licking of ice cream and wearing of oversize shoes seem joined by a disproportion between need and means inherent in the Italian character.) Stanza six is a collage of noisy, shoving image fragments; and the poem as a whole is a collage of images with little—for Mina Loy—interpretation. She has restrained the I, as Marinetti demands, to focus on the dynamism of the street.

"The Costa San Giorgio" with its demonstration of Italian and poetic vitality is one of Loy's most impressive poems because it successfully employs the image to depict the impact of the sensuous world upon consciousness. Throughout her poetry success is conditional upon the power of the image to rescue metaphysical explorations from the grey mists of abstraction. Because of the importance of the image, it seems worthwhile to conclude the discussion of "The Costa San Giorgio" by looking behind Marinetti to Bergson in order to complete the metaphysical and aesthetic basis of Loy's use of the image in a poetic milieu energized by its possibilities.

According to Bergson, a disconnected series of images is the means by which the self is brought to the intuition of its essence

—its duration: "No image can replace the intuition of duration, but many diverse images, borrowed from very different orders of things, may, by the convergence of their action, direct consciousness to the precise point where there is a certain intuition to be seized. By choosing images as dissimilar as possible, we shall prevent any one of them from usurping the place of the intuition it is intended to call up, since it would then be driven away at once by its rivals."[13] Such a collage of images increasingly structures Mina Loy's poems. The image is an extension of the shaping I-eye, rather than its diminution, as it strives to evoke and evaluate the essence of a person, object, or situation by presenting multiple perspectives of the subject. A conduit to the intuition, the image is often effectively alternated with the abstractions of the intellect. However, Loy tends to become didactic and abstract, a weakness cited by T. S. Eliot in regard to "Human Cylinders" (*ca.* 1914/1917): "She needs the support of the image, even if only as the instant point of departure; in this poem she becomes abstract, and the word separates from the thing."[14] Loy appears to have been aware of this weakness, for as her poetry moves into the 1920s images dominate or supplant abstractions. Arranged in collage structures suggested by the theory and practice of Apollinaire, Marinetti, and Bergson and encouraged undoubtedly by the attention of English and American poets to Imagism (Loy was too discursive and abstract to be an Imagist), the images of her poems convey the flux of life and the richness of her intuition.

II   *The "Love Songs"*   In pressing the material to derive its essence, matter becomes deformed.
—"Aphorisms on Futurism"

13. Henri Bergson, *An Introduction to Metaphysics*, trans. T. E. Hulme (Indianapolis: Bobbs-Merrill, 1955), 27–28. Raymond, *From Baudelaire to Surrealism*, 62–63 and 117–18, discusses the influence of Bergson's ideas on the literature of his time.

14. T. S. Apteryx [Eliot], "Observations," *Egoist*, V (1918), 70.

In the *Love Songs*, or *Songs to Joannes* (1915–1917),[15] Mina Loy unites her most innovative structural experiments with her bleakest examination of female selfhood. The conjunction typifies the modernist effort to find a more organic relation between subject and structure than that offered by old poetic forms. Loy's analysis of failed love requires, as the epigraph to this section suggests, radical deformations of line and image. The result is a collage of fragments of body and mind; religious and romantic values; and past, present, and future times. The accomplishment of fitting form to experience merits the *Love Songs* consideration with such modernist efforts to structure new perceptions of self and world as Gertrude Stein's *Tender Buttons* (1914), T. S. Eliot's *The Long Song of J. Alfred Prufrock* (1915) and *The Waste Land* (1922), William Carlos Williams' *Kora in Hell* (1920), Ezra Pound's *Hugh Selwyn Mauberley* (1920), and Marianne Moore's "Marriage" (1923).

The similarities between the *Love Songs* and *Prufrock* are especially useful in placing Loy's poems in their literary and cultural context. Although completed in 1911, *Prufrock* like the *Love Songs* was not published until 1915. This concurrence eliminates the possibility of influence but underscores the similarity of the poems' response to the cultural and artistic moment. Structurally both the *Love Songs* and *Prufrock* embody the movement of consciousness in disjunctive forms (the *Love Songs* even more closely resemble the collage structure of *The Waste Land*). The titles and internal allusions of both invite ironic comparison of these mod-

15. Mina Loy refers to the incomplete collection of poems as the *Love Songs*, but she anticipates in a letter to Van Vechten (*ca.* summer, 1915) that the complete poems will become the volume *Songs to Joannes*. This wish is fulfilled when the thirty-four poems are published in *Others* (April, 1917). However, earlier publications of the first four poems in *Others* (July, 1915) and the *Others* anthology for 1916 are titled *Love Songs*. In her correspondence Loy uses both titles; and representative selections published in *Lunar Baedeker* and *Lunar Baedeker & Time-Tables*, where presumably her wishes are followed, are titled *Love Songs*. Thus, I refer to the poems as the *Love Songs*, their original, most commonly used, and most well-known title.

ern love songs to their heroic predecessors, and both Loy's I and Prufrock are descendants of Jules Laforgue's Pierrot, who offers songs of love to a cold moon. Laforgue is of course the significant ancestor in a number of ways. Both the *Love Songs* and *Prufrock* employ Laforguian imagery, and the I, who is not provided with the common modernist mask, like Prufrock speaks colloquially with the self-deprecatory irony of Pierrot. Like Pierrot, the I and Prufrock discover cultural decay and individual (especially sexual) inadequacy via the treacherous passages of love. The I confronts the world more aggressively than Prufrock, but her defeat in an image of crucifixion is as complete as his drowning in an ocean of self-doubt and fear.

The I of the *Love Songs* is the victim of an un-Prufrockian masculine assertiveness and egotism epitomized in Loy's experience by the Futurists and stereotyped in literature by the figure of Don Juan (or Don Giovanni), who in the *Love Songs* becomes Joannes. She does not name the Futurists, but their opinions on love and women are important to the *Love Songs*. Love has introduced the I to Futurist mating stripped of religious and social sanctions and emotional security. Love is only sex, and sex is ephemeral physical pleasure (poem XIV):

> No love   or the other thing
> Only the impact of lighted bodies
> Knocking sparks off each other
> In chaos

The mysterious "other thing" may be hatred, love's opposite; perhaps it is procreation. The Futurists, Loy gibes in the satire "Lions' Jaws," hoped for "Man's immediate agamogenesis."

That the *Love Songs* like many of Mina Loy's early poems respond to arrogant Futurist masculinity seems clear, but it is unnecessary as well as difficult to pinpoint the source of the bitterness which inspired them. She suffered a romantic disappointment sometime between 1913 and 1915, but on the manuscript of the first four poems, in reference to poem IV, she says "these are the subconscious impressions of 8 years ago! What were they—the butterfly [poem III] is the other day."[16] The poems probably synthesize this worldly woman's long search for an ideal love.

Autobiographical comment more successfully explains Loy's conception of the structure of the poems. Letters to Van Vechten indicate that most of the poems were written by 1915. In March she tells him that there were to have been twenty-one poems but that she only wrote seventeen—"the love having spent itself." Fear of personal revelation or public hostility to the poems' sexual honesty causes her to add that they are of "no interest to the public—I may send them to you for your eye alone." Inspiration returns, however, for finally there are thirty-four poems and she is eager for a publisher. In late summer she notes the major division in the sequence: "All the first were in red hot agony in the traditional recuperation in the country—and the rest —settled cerebral—except that inimitable reminder—

> The moon is cold
> Joannes
> Where the Mediterranean— — — —"[17]

She explains in another letter that the "whole will make a progression of realisations—crescendo and transcendo!"

The narrative unraveled by the poems moves from "red hot

16. Mina Loy, *Love Songs* I–IV (MS in Carl Van Vechten Papers, Collection of American Literature, Beinecke Rare Book and Manuscript Library, Yale University).

17. The image of the Mediterranean, poem XXXII of the *Love Songs*, probably comes from Jules Laforgue's "Au Large":
> Comme la nuit est lointainement pleine
> De silencieuse infinité claire!
> Pas le moindre écho des gens de la terre,
> Sous la Lune méditerranéenne!

("How the night is vastly full / Of calm and clear infinity; / Not the least echo of the earth's people, / Under the Mediterranean moon!") The translations provided herein are my own literal translations.

agony" (sublimated in psychic animals) to cerebral analysis, a variation of the flux between image and abstraction in "Parturition" and "The Effectual Marriage." But narrative progression blurs before the tumultuous intermingling of past and present, fact and the hallucinations of the subconscious. In depicting this clash of diverse times and levels of experience Loy utilizes the juxtaposition and typographical irregularity of "The Costa San Giorgio," but the juxtapositions of the *Love Songs* are heterogeneous and, hence, more abrupt and disconnected. The fragmentation reflects cultural disintegration and the I's mental confusion rather than universal dynamism. Each of the *Love Songs* rearranges the fragments of love: sometimes in coherent, autonomous images; sometimes in complex collages. As a whole the poems form a Futurist collage of thirty-four perspectives on failed love. "Coloured   glass," the last line of poem I, introduces the kaleidoscope analogy; the poems are to be understood as shifting configurations of symbolic colors and image fragments. The most important of the latter are cosmological images (sun, moon, stars), time images (day, noon, dawn, midnight, clockwork), animal and biological images and terms, and images of light, vision, vegetation, flight, deity, the house, and mechanization. To completely understand a word or image the reader must have in mind its referents in the other thirty-three poems. Not all the poems employ fragmentation and most have some autonomy, but all increase in intelligibility when placed in the larger intricate pattern of themes and images. This exaggerated reflexiveness of language is another instance of the spatialization Joseph Frank cites as characteristic of modern literature and its sense of the disharmonious relation between self and world.[18]

In the *Love Songs* spatialization reflects the I's inability to attain selfhood, the "covered entrance to infinity." She has wanted to assert and define the self as Futurism and Bergsonian meta-

18. Joseph Frank, *The Widening Gyre: Crisis and Mastery in Modern Literature* (Bloomington: Indiana University Press, 1963), 13 and *passim*.

physics encouraged her to do. But instead of experiencing a continuous, spontaneous, and sexually luminescent self-expansion
in time (*i.e.*, Futurist dynamism or Bergsonian duration), she
knows fragmentation and stasis. She rearranges the fragments of
love in each poem, but she cannot escape the closed circle formed
by the shifting of these fragments. She is frozen in space, unable
to find the answer that would break the circle of her despair. The
image of this stasis in poem xxxi recalls Eliot's comatose "patient
etherised upon a table": "Crucifixion / Wracked arms / Index extremities / In vacuum / To the unbroken fall." This physical and
psychic paralysis is intensified by the startling images of sexual
disillusion and guilt which dominate the first half of the *Love
Songs*. Loy explains to Van Vechten that these fantastic figures
"came straight out of my subconsciousness," and indeed their
disturbing forcefulness lies in the surrealistic link they forge between sexuality and the psyche. In addition to their subconscious
origin and grotesque shapes, they share with Surrealist painting
the sharp-edged contours of magical realism.

As a preface to further discussion it is useful to note Loy's concern for the layout of the poems. She writes to Van Vechten, "If
you wanted me to be a happy woman for five minutes or more,
you would get Songs for Joannes published for me—all together
—printed on one side of each page only—and a large round in
the middle of the blank reverse of each page—and one whole
entirely blank page with *nothing* on it between the first and the
second parts—(pause in between moods)—the dedication 'TO
YOU.'" [19] Loy was in New York when the complete poems appeared (the first four had initiated *Others* in 1915),[20] and she

19. The proposed dedicatory poem "To You" appears in *Others*, July, 1916. It
is an elusive evocation of the loved one in the context of the city.
20. In a letter to Van Vechten (July, 1915) Loy cites errors in the first *Others*
printing of poem I: "Silting the appraisable" has been misprinted "Sitting the
appraisable"; "There are suspect places" should read "These are suspect
places."

probably edited the April, 1917, issue of *Others* which comprised them.[21] She omitted the blank pages and dedicatory poem, undoubtedly because of the magazine's sorry finances, but each poem possesses sufficient white space to emphasize its visual properties. The first four poems, the most well known and most "modern" of the *Love Songs*, follow as published in 1917:

> Spawn   of   Fantasies
> Silting the appraisable
> Pig Cupid   his rosy snout
> Rooting erotic garbage
> "Once upon a time"
> Pulls a weed   white and star-topped
> Among wild oats   sewn in mucous-membrane
>
> I would   an   eye in a Bengal light
> Eternity in a sky-rocket
> Contellations in an ocean
> Whose rivers run no fresher
> Than a trickle of saliva
> These   are suspect places
>
> I must live in my lantern
> Trimming subliminal flicker
> Virginal   to the bellows
> Of Experience
>   Coloured   glass
>
>   II
>
>   The skin-sack
> In which a wanton duality
> Packed
> All the completions of my infructuous impulses
> Something the shape of a man
> To the casual vulgarity of the merely observant
> More of a clock-work mechanism
> Running down against time

21. In *Others*, May–June, 1916, Kreymborg announces that subsequent issues will have guest editors.

To which I am not paced
    My finger-tips are numb from fretting your hair
A God's door-mat
                    On the threshold of your mind

III

We might have coupled
In the bed-ridden monopoly of a moment
Or broken flesh with one another
At the profane communion table
Where wine is spill't on promiscuous lips

We might have given birth to a butterfly
With the daily-news
Printed in blood on its wings

IV

Once in a mezzanino
The starry ceiling
Vaulted an unimaginable family
Bird-like abortions
With human throats
And Wisdom's eyes
Who wore lamp-shade red dresses
And woolen hair
One bore a baby
In a padded porte-enfant
Tied with a sarsenet ribbon
To her goose's wings

But for the abominable shadows
I would have lived
Among their fearful furniture
To teach them to tell me their secrets
Before I guessed
—Sweeping the brood clean out

Poem I, above all others, deserves consideration for its structural innovation, complexity, and thematic centrality. Image follows image in a collage that both originates and concludes the narrative. Few are the images or motifs in later poems that do not lead back to it. The poem opens in a garden of love, not an elegantly landscaped formal garden with marble cupids presiding over sentimental rendezvous, but a garden of sensuality pillaged by the lascivious Pig Cupid. Pig Cupid may have originated in a line from Laforgue's "Locutions des Pierrots" (XII): "Les dieux s'en vont; plus que des hures."[22] In Loy's poems of female selfhood, he represents male arrogance and the failure of romantic love, as well as sexual disillusion and suppressed guilt. He is both the loved one and the experience of love. The erotic garbage he swills is love's wreckage. Ironically, the weed contaminating the innocent promiscuity of the loved one's wild oats is the I. Her romantic aspirations—"white and star-topped," which left her susceptible to betrayal, reverse their value in the new sexual code. She has been transformed from blossom to weed. A similar reversal runs throughout the other poems as traditional romantic and religious values become immoral because they violate the loved one's independence and a new and as yet unintelligible cosmic order.

As previously noted, time in this love story is spatialized: a chaotic mingling of present despair with fragments of the past. '"Once upon a time"' recalls an earlier time when the uninitiated woman viewed love as a fairy-tale romance and was repaid for her illusions with the deflowering that transformed her into a weed. '"Once upon a time"' she and a purposeful universe moved in a harmony that the failure of love has destroyed. Personal time has disintegrated into bits and pieces: '"Once upon a time,"' the treacherous subjunctives "I would" and "We might have," and the desperate imperative "I must."

In contrast to the spatialized chaos of personal time, the poems offer evolutionary progress which, according to Marinetti, would

22. Marinetti's adaptation of Laforgue's line for the title *Les Dieux s'en vont, d'Annunzio reste* (Paris: 1908) may also lie behind Pig Cupid.

release men and women from their traditional sexual roles, and the time, or rhythm, of biological instinct and decay. Contrary to Marinetti's optimism, the *Love Songs* disclose that when men and women cut themselves loose from romantic love they do not evolve to a higher plane of human existence but regress to animalistic sexual instinct. This regression is a spiritually unsatisfying alternative to obsolete teleological progression that gave purpose to human love.

Biological time, implicit in the animal imagery of poem i, dominates poem ii, where the I is out of step with the loved one's "clock-work mechanism" (a phallic "skin-sack"). Having evolved to a plane of sexual irresponsibility, he becomes a biological mechanism "Running down against time" to which the I is not "paced." This paradox of a biological/mechanical humanity recurs in poem xxv, where nature's deceptive beauty entices the lovers to a dance that transforms them into machines:

> Licking the Arno
> The little rosy
> Tongue of Dawn
> Interferes with our eyelashes
>
> ——————————
>
> We twiddle to it
> Round and round
> Faster
> And turn into machines
>
> Till the sun
> Subsides in shining
> Melts some of us
> Into abysmal pigeon-holes
> Passion has bored
> In warmth
>
> Some few of us
> Grow to the level of cool plains
> Cutting our foot-hold
> With steel eyes

Of the animal images (reminders of biological time) bombarding the I from the subconscious, Pig Cupid "Silting the appraisable" with his sexual sediment represents the obliterating power of sexuality dodging repression in grotesque fantasies. He originates in the spaces of the opening line, the abyss of the subconscious where sexual desire and spiritual aspiration foment images of disillusion and guilt. These spaces may also visualize pauses of the intuition—the mind's hesitation before it plunges into the subconscious or, elsewhere, outward into the universe in search of the truth of its being.

The opening images of lewd sensuality and biological time give way to images of an ideal time—"I would." The ideal is also sexual, imaged at the outset as beautiful moment of orgasm: "I would   an   eye in a Bengal light / Eternity in a sky-rocket / Constellations in an ocean." Arranged in the rapid-fire order advocated by Marinetti and Bergson, these images are adequate unto themselves, but an understanding of their adaptation of Bergsonian imagery helps to measure the I's fall from the ideal to the actual.

Bergson says in *Creative Evolution* that the quality of human life depends on consciousness, "the living being's power of choice" —his ability to invent and to act freely. To lack consciousness is to be an animal of routine, an automaton. Consciousness ought to represent a balance of intellect and intuition, but the latter "is a lamp almost extinguished, which only glimmers now and then, for a few moments at most. But it glimmers wherever a vital interest is at stake."[23] As "an   eye   in a Bengal light" (a blue light used for signaling or illumination), the I knows a moment of rare perfect consciousness in which she escapes the animality and automatism represented by Pig Cupid: she communicates with the cosmos and projects brilliantly her realized self. In terms of the

23. Henri Bergson, *Creative Evolution*, trans. Arthur Mitchell (New York: Modern Library, 1944), 287–88, 291–92.

poem's color symbolism, the blueness of a Bengal light is the divinity of perfect human love, in contrast to Pig Cupid's lascivious rosiness.

The short-lived skyrocket—Bergson's image for "supra-consciousness," the vital current and evolutionary force creating and impelling life—images a moment so intense that it encompasses eternity.[24] With the implied contrast of self and the rocket she "would" be, the I defines her earth-bound submission to chaos, animality, and automatism. The rocket is also the most vivid of the poems' many images of flight, symbol of psychic and sexual freedom. It is a phallic image possessing aggressive, directional vitality. (As a mechanical image the rocket ironically contrasts the Futurist technological ideal to the "clock-work" sexual reality of Futurist masculinity.) The water image juxtaposed to the skyrocket symbolizes female sexuality, placid and all-encompassing. In the image "Constellations in an ocean" the masculine and feminine principles unite as the sparks from the skyrocket glow like stars to transpose the lovers and the universe into a moment of orgasmic completion. The rapid sequence of disconnected images, moving from the contracted intensity of the eye to the expansive constellations, enacts the excited crescendo of orgasm. Again this sexual imagery draws upon Bergson, who characterizes consciousness as a "beneficent fluid," the "ocean of life" from which humanity draws its strength. Hence in the image "Constellations in an ocean" the I experiences cosmic consciousness. However, she cannot sustain the ideal and her excitement fades to the characteristic deflationary rhythm of the *Love Songs*. In mockery of Bergsonian optimism the ocean recedes to a river, Bergson's image of duration,[25] and then dissipates to a "trickle of saliva," sordid biological process. Such sordidness has been suggested by "spawn," "silting," "mucous membrane," and it recurs

24. *Ibid.*, 271–74.
25. *Ibid.*, 210, 294.

in "skin-sack," "the scum of the white street" (vii), "spermato-zoa" (ix), "the weak eddy / Of your drivelling humanity" (xv), and "cymophonous sweat" (xxviii). The treacherous dissipation of sexual intensity and romantic beauty produces the space of "These   are suspect places." The I hesitates before again daring the abyss that surrounds the effort to love.

The final cluster of images marks the triumph of discretion. An urgent "I must" supplants the hopeful "I would" and the I retreats from another miscalculation. Love has initiated her to the necessity of husbanding her vital intuitional light whose ex-pansion proved disastrous. "Subliminal flicker" introduces the motif of diminished light that recurs in the image of the I as the "candle ends" of the flame that led the loved one to knowledge and in the flickering, ephemeral light of mating glowworms:

VIII

I am the jealous store-house of the candle-ends
That lit your adolescent learning
————————————

Behind God's eyes
There might
Be other lights

XIV

Today
Everlasting   passing   apparent   imperceptible
To you
I bring the nascent virginity of
—Myself   for the moment

No love   or the other thing
Only the impact of lighted bodies
Knocking sparks off each other
In chaos

Remy de Gourmont, a contemporary author Mina Loy had un-doubtedly read, explains in *The Natural Philosophy of Love* (1903) the intent of the glowworm image. He says that for purposes of procreation glowworms are attracted to each other by their phosphorescent wings; then "after coupling they fade as lamps when extinguished. . . . The fading light is symbolic of the destiny of nearly all insects, and of many animals also; coupling accomplished, their reason for being disappears and life vanishes from them."[26] The I of the *Love Songs* has learned that her vital light was only bait in the sexual game.

But while "lantern / Trimming subliminal flicker" develops the biological and light imagery of the poem, it also alludes to myths that explain the I's predicament. We remember the parable of the virgins (Matthew 25:1–13) who took their lamps and went out to await the coming of the bridegroom. When "at midnight there was a cry made, Behold, the bridegroom cometh; go ye out to meet him," the "virgins arose, and trimmed their lamps." Five finding they had come without oil went to obtain it. While they were gone the bridegroom appeared and the five wise virgins went into the marriage feast with him, "and the door was shut." The five foolish, returning, also sought admittance but the Lord answered them, "I know you not. Watch therefore, for ye know neither the day nor the hour wherein the Son of man cometh." The parable admonishes preparedness, for men "know neither the day nor the hour" of the second coming of Christ and with him the kingdom of heaven. It also reassures the prepared who have waited patiently that their faith will not be disappointed.[27]

The I has been one of the unprepared virgins, deceived by the doctrines of romantic and religious love. Religion's responsibility for her ignorance and subsequent disillusion is suggested again in poem XIII: "Where two or three are welded together / They shall become god." Here the expectation that earthly love

26. Remy de Gourmont, *The Natural Philosophy of Love*, trans. Ezra Pound (New York: Boni and Liveright, 1922), 41–42.

27. George Arthur Buttrick, *et al.* (eds.), *The Interpreter's Bible* (New York: Abingdon Press, 1951), 555–58.

will open the door to heavenly love appears in a variation of
Matthew 18:20: "For where two or three are gathered together
in my name, there am I in the midst of them." Loy's substitution
of "welded" for "gathered" suggests that traditional expectations of love have failed because the lovers are merely machines
of instinct, joined by the fires of lust. The juxtaposition of Jaco-
bean English and colloquial phrasing emphasizes the difference
between religious promise and reality: "Oh that's right / Keep
away from me   Please give me a push / Don't let me understand you   Don't realise me."

Most of the *Love Songs* are flashbacks to the search for the
loved one and admittance to his house and, thereby, to the kingdom of heaven. Kaleidoscopic fragments of house imagery recall
"The Effectual Marriage" and "At the Door of the House,"
poems in which the house and its door represent the hope and
failure of love as well as the sexual body. In the *Love Songs* poem
II images the I as fretting the lover's hair, "A God's door-mat /
On the threshold of your mind." Poem XVII like poem IV places
the I within a room of mental torment (a room she would like to
sweep clean):

> I don't care
> Where the legs of the legs of the furniture are walking to
> Or what is hidden in the shadows they stride
> Or what would look at me
> If the shutters were not shut
> Red   a warm colour on the battle-field
> Heavy on my knees as a counterpane
> Count counter
> I counted   the fringe of the towel
> Till two tassels clinging together
> Let the square room fall away
> From a round vacuum
> Dilating with my breath

In poems V through VII the I pursues her lover through
house-filled streets:

V

Midnight empties the street
Of all but us
Three
I am undecided which way back
                    To the left a boy
—One wing has been washed in the rain
   The other will never be clean any more—
Pulling door-bells to remind
Those that are snug
                    To the right a haloed ascetic
                    Threading houses
Probes wounds for souls
—The poor can't wash in hot water—
And I dont know which turning to take
Since you got home to yourself—first

VI

I know the Wire-Puller intimately
And if it were not for the people
On whom you keep one eye
You could look straight at me
And Time would be set back

VII

My pair of feet
Smack the flag-stones
That are something left over from your walking
The wind stuffs the scum of the white street
Into my lungs and my nostrils
Exhilarated birds
Prolonging flight into the night
Never reaching—————

In poem xxviii she climbs endless steps to the loved one's
house: "Unthinkable   that white over there / ——— Is smoke
from your house." In viii she is the "jealous store-house" of his
adolescence, an image completed in xxxi, where as a caryatid,
pillar of the ancient house of the gods, she is blasted off her
foundations and thrown into cosmic darkness:

Crucifixion
Of an illegal ego's
Eclosion
On your equilibrium
Caryatid   of an idea

Crucifixion
Wracked arms
Index extremities
In vacuum
To the unbroken fall

Here again de Gourmont may provide the gloss of this image. In "Women and Language" (1901) he uses the caryatid to represent the feminine ideal: "The role of women in the work of civilization is so great that it would scarcely be an exaggeration to say that the structure is built on the shoulders of these frail caryatids."[28] In this context Mina Loy's caryatid carries with her ruin the whole of Western civilization.

In short, the I has subscribed to the Judaic-Christian world view constructed as a shield against cosmic darkness. It sanctified human mating and directed it toward a more perfect existence. "Our daily deaths," as poem xxvii refers to life (and its moments of orgasm), were constructed as a progression toward spiritual reward. The loved one's sexual irresponsibility wrecks the religious valuation of life, as it had the romantic, and the I recognizes that the old explanations are inadequate: "What guaranty / For the proto-form / We fumble / Our souvenir ethics to" (xxx). Purpose and order vanish and the I tumbles into the cosmic abyss against which love and religion, in an earlier time, would have protected her. The extent of her despair is reflected in the blasphemous (Decadent) image of the unholy eucharist in poem iii. Rather than admitting the lovers to the kingdom of heaven, love defiles them. "Coupled" connotes mechanical and

28. Glenn S. Burne (ed. and trans.), *Remy de Gourmont: Selected Writings* (Ann Arbor: University of Michigan Press, 1966), 130.

animal union, while "bed-ridden" suggests sickness, "monopoly" domination, and "broken" violence.

   The failure of religious love may be due in part to the I's sacri-
legious deification of the loved one. In poem II his hair is a
"God's door-mat," and in VIII he appears as a god nourished by
other female lights than the I's wearied candle-ends. In XXII his
absence, godlike, denies her grace: "In ways without you / I go /
Gracelessly / As things go." The terminology is confused in XV.
Disillusioned with mortal men who did not live up to her fantasies of godliness, the I worshiped the loved one for his "Su-
perhumanness," but this earthly superlative deflates, as did the
cosmic immensity of poem I:

> Seldom   Trying for Love
> Fantasy dealt them out as gods
> Two or three men   looked only human
>
> But you alone
> Superhuman   apparently
> I had to be caught in the weak eddy
> Of your drivelling humanity
>   To love you most

   As a god the loved one is also a distortion of Cupid (Pig Cupid), whose love affair with Psyche helps to measure the I's fall
from the ideal. Symbol of life, breath, and the soul, Psyche appears in poem III in the traditional form of the butterfly. In the
mythic tale of Apuleius, the beautiful Psyche rouses the jealousy
of Venus, who demands that her son Cupid cause Psyche to fall
in love with "the vilest of men." However, Cupid himself is
smitten and he wafts Psyche away to a sumptuous palace. He
visits her only at night and she is forbidden to look at him or to
seek his identity. Goaded by the veiled malice of her sisters, the
naïve Psyche takes a lamp and looks at Cupid, finds him exceed-
ingly handsome, and falls passionately in love. But a drop of hot
oil falls on him and he awakens and flees to his mother's house.
Conscious now of love, Psyche pursues Cupid and is forced by a

wrathful Venus to perform nearly impossible tasks. Cupid still very much in love, enlists the aid of his father Jove, who gives Psyche immortality and commands her marriage to Cupid. Psyche and Cupid have a daughter Pleasure.[29] In the *Love Songs* the I, carrying the lamp of her suppressed desire, has tried to penetrate the loved one's "inviolate ego," to know him (xii–xvi). He flees such revelation and she becomes a slave of love, pursuing him through dark, nightmarish streets (v–vii). But the loved one is Pig Cupid, not Cupid, and no Jove intervenes to provide a happy ending. The offspring of this couple is not pleasure but "Bird-like abortions" (iv). The beautiful, divine self that love "might have" given birth to is defiled by the blood of sexual battle and the crass sensuality of the tabloids (iii): "We might have given birth to a butterfly / With the daily-news / Printed in blood on its wings." If the butterfly in another of its symbolic functions is the perfect aesthetic object, the disfigured butterfly images the distortion of form required to shape this unhappy love affair into literature.

Numerous other winged creatures, variations of the butterfly and Pig Cupid, flitter through the *Love Songs*. Like Pig Cupid, the winged street urchin (v) profanes the god of love. The ambiguous "Exhilarated birds" (vii) seem to represent mental and physical vitality smothered by the sexual "scum of the white street." In their transformation to "abysmal pigeon-holes" (xxv), the lovers lose their humanity because they have yielded to sexual desire. The carelessly strewn feathers of the badminton-like shuttlecock and battledore are the trivial litter left after the sexual game (x): "Shuttle-cock and battle-door / A little pink-love / And feathers are strewn." And glowworms and fireflies (xiv, xix) image ephemeral sexual conjunctions. Recognizing that she will never be the healthy butterfly, or even a briefly glimmering

29. Erich Neumann, *Amor and Psyche: The Psychic Development of the Feminine, A Commentary on the Tale of Apuleius*, trans. Ralph Manheim (New York: Pantheon Books, 1956), 3–53.

firefly, the I dismisses the possibility of flight (xx): "Let Joy go solace-winged / To flutter whom she may concern." Her effort at flight has been an "eclosion" (xxxi): insect-like, she has struggled free of her pupal case of romantic illusion only to plunge in "unbroken fall" through the vacuum of a meaningless existence.

As the modern unsuccessful and unredeemed Psyche, to return to the opening poem, the I has been subjected to the "bellows / Of Experience." Buffeted and disfigured in the fires fanned by the bellows, she wishes now to remain "virginal" to love. The ambiguous image "Coloured   glass" represents both the ignorance she once knew and the ignorance to which she wishes to return. She entered love with naïve faith in her power to shape the world that might have derived from the "Aphorisms" : "Not to be a cipher in your ambient, / But to color your ambient with your preferences." She discovers, however, as the "Aphorisms" warn, that "believing yourself free—your least conception is colored by the pigment of retrograde superstitions." Romantic and religious ideals prevent her from coloring the world realistically; her illusions toss her into the fires of lust where the colored glass of love is "smelt" to whiteness.

"Coloured   glass" sets in motion the kaleidoscope of color whose blurring, or heating, to whiteness charts the evolution of the I's knowledge. The uninitiated young lovers look upon a glorious world of "coloured voices," the promised land (ix):

> When we lifted
> Our eye-lids on Love
> A cosmos
> Of coloured voices
> And laughing honey
>
> And spermatozoa
> At the core of Nothing
> In the milk of the Moon

Loveliness deflates to "spermatozoa" and nothingness, as well as a "little pink-love" and then to the onion of poem xi:

> Dear one   at your mercy
> Our Universe
> Is only
> A colorless onion
> You derobe
> Sheath by sheath
>   Remaining
> A disheartening odour
> About your nervy hands

Among the fragments of colored glass greenness symbolizes nature's beauty untainted by human desire and meanness. Nature's center is the indifferent, life-giving sun. If the I could move in harmony with the laws of sunlight, if she could de-evolve to a state of nature, she would escape her torment. The prayer she offers to the laws of evolution and "unnatural" selection asks that human qualities be bred out of man and woman, leaving them only their natural functions (xxix):

> Evolution   fall foul of
> Sexual equality
> Prettily miscalculate
> Similitude
> Unnatural selection
> Breed such sons and daughters
> As shall jibber at each other
> Uninterpretable cryptonyms
> Under the moon
>
> Give them some way of braying brassily
> For caressive calling
> Or to homophonous hiccoughs
> Transpose the laugh
> Let them suppose that tears
> Are snowdrops or molasses
> Or anything
> Than human insufficiencies
> Begging dorsal vertebrae

This prayer ironically endorses Marinetti's call (in *War, the World's Only Hygiene*) for a "nonhuman type": "If we grant the truth of Lamarck's transformational hypothesis we must admit that we look for the creation of a nonhuman type in whom moral suffering, goodness of heart, affection, and love, those sole corrosive poisons of inexhaustible vital energy, sole interrupters of our powerful bodily electricity, will be abolished."[30]

Nature can also be a restorative (we remember Loy's mention of the "traditional recuperation in the country"). The short, disconnected lines and images (in the manner of Laforgue's "Dimanches") of poem XIX resemble a formula, a medicinal prescription for love's victims:[31]

> Nothing so conserving
> As cool cleaving
> Note of the Q H U
> Clear carving
> Breath-giving
> Pollen smelling
> Space
>
> White telling
> Of slaking
> Drinkable
> Through fingers
> Running water
> Grass haulms
> Grow to
>
> Leading astray
> Of fireflies
> Aerial quadrille
> Bouncing
> Off one another
> Again conjoining
> In recaptured pulses
> Of light

The "cerebral forager" of XXII images the I who, in a state of recuperative retrospection, combs nature for explanations of her

30. Flint (ed.), *Marinetti: Selected Writings*, 91.
31. See Kenneth Rexroth, "The Influence of French Poetry on American," in *Assays* (Norfolk, Conn.: New Directions, 1961), 156. Rexroth quotes Wyndham

disappointment: "Green things grow / Salads / For the cerebral / Forager's revival." Nature's indifference to mankind appears in the image of the lover in xix as a faded glowworm: "You too / Had something / At that time / Of a green-lit glow-worm / ———— / Yet slowly drenched / To raylessness / In rain." Nature is a pornographist angered by human efforts to impose moral order on her (xxvi):

> Shedding our petty pruderies
> From slit eyes
>
> We sidle up
> To Nature
> ——— that irate pornographist

Quite simply, nature is blind to human needs: "For the blind eyes / That Nature knows us with / And the most of Nature   is green" (xxx).

Contrasted to nature's indifferent green beauty is the "red hot agony" of passion. The violence and anguish of sexual conflict appear in the bloody butterfly, the red dresses of the "bird-like abortions" (iv), "humid carnage" (xii), and the red battlefield (xvii). The rosy colored dawn of epic tradition receives a lewd twist in the "rosy / Tongue of Dawn" (xxv), and of course there is the rosy snout of Pig Cupid.

The whiteness that dissipates passion and romance to a "little pink-love" originates in the false romantic ideals engendered by white lunar light, the "milk of the Moon." Moonlight shapes a world of colored voices and lights along the Arno, but like the "white and star-topped" weed of Pig Cupid's garden, this beauty is disfigured by sexual reality. Moonlight deceptively draws the I into cosmic blackness: the dark, empty streets of midnight (v, vii), nightmares (xxi), and a frozen night landscape (xxiii):

Lewis on the Laforguian manner: "'Describe human beings as though they were machines, landscapes as though they were chemical formulas, inanimate objects as though they were alive.'"

XXI

I store up nights against you
Heavy with shut-flower's nightmares
— — — — — — — — — — —
Stack noons
Curled to the solitaire
Core of the
Sun

XXIII

Laughter in solution
Stars in a stare
Irredeemable pledges
Of pubescent consummations
Rot
To the recurrent moon
Bleach
To the pure white
Wickedness of pain

Moonlight becomes saliva, driveling humanity, and the scum of the street through which the I pursues the loved one to his house—from which pours white smoke. Moonlight leads the I into the fires of love and a vision of cosmic purposelessness: "Nucleus   Nothing / Inconceivable concept" (xxvii). An image of sexual intercourse leaves no ambiguity as to the source of this transforming fire (xxviii):

Coloured   conclusions
Smelt   to synthetic
Whiteness
Of my
Emergence
And I am burnt quite white
In the climacteric
Withdrawal of your sun

The lover has been, in his sexual potency, her warming, life-sustaining sun, and without him she discovers and mirrors universal emptiness (xxvii):

> The contents
> Of our ephemeral conjunction
> In aloofness from Much
> Flowed to approachment of — — — —
> NOTHING
> There was a man and a woman
> In the way

The last three *Love Songs*, reflections upon disfigured love, distance the I from her pain. In XXXII the lunar light has been extinguished, along with innocence and joy. A cold moon no longer deceives the I, but neither does it hold out the expectation of earthly or heavenly bliss. The I has fallen into unmasked reality:

> The moon is cold
> Joannes
> Where the Mediterranean — — — — —

Poem XXXIII concludes the theme of an evolutionary process that has made traditional views of love obsolete and destructive:

> The prig of passion — — — —
> To your professorial paucity
>
> Proto-plasm was raving mad
> Evolving us — — —

Products of a mad protoplasm, the lovers seem unfit for the general course of evolution toward sexual independence and equality; or, since the loved one has seemed to represent the new order, the image of a mad protoplasm may suggest that the lovers have been propelled into incompatible evolutionary currents. A "prig of passion," the I has too fastidiously observed the code of romantic love; while the loved one's "professorial paucity"[32] suggests the aloofness and egotism of which she ac-

---

32. "Professorial" departs from the poem's imagery, but it is autobiographically interesting to note that in "The Effectual Marriage" the husband, Miovanni, is a scholar closeted in his study. Giovanni Papini, who may have been at least a partial inspiration for the *Love Songs*, was a man of letters.

cuses him in xiii: "Oh that's right / Keep away from me   Please give me a push / Don't let me understand you   Don't realise me." "Prig" contains and recalls "pig" and also concludes the clown imagery of the slit-eyed clown (xxvi) who dares the devious ways of nature by sidling up to her and of the Laforguian foetal buffoons who fulfill archetypal patterns they are helpless to alter (xxx): "In some / Prenatal plagiarism / Foetal buffoons / Caught tricks — — — — — / / From archetypal pantomime / Stringing emotions / Looped aloft." Thus, aspirations unfit to an advanced state of human evolution have reduced the I to clownishness.

The I has been trapped. She realizes that romantic guises have been used to breed human types who scorn the old romantic notions. She herself is a throwback to an earlier type. Here de Gourmont again illuminates the basic irony of the *Love Songs*. In explaining the role of sexual selection within evolution he says that some aspects of the selection process, like mating songs, no longer serve their original function. For example, the incessant song of the male grasshopper falls upon the nearly deaf ears of his mates. However, he continues, "the unending song may have been useful at a time when the sexes lived separate, and may have remained as evidence of ancient customs. It is moreover a commonly observed fact that activities long survive the period of their utility. Man and all animals are full of maniac gestures whose movement is only explicable on the hypothesis that it had once a different intention." [33] In an age of (Futurist) sexual equality human love songs, like the chirping of the grasshopper, are antiquated, "maniac gestures."

Accordingly, the final poem, "Love — — — the preeminent literateur," mocks the poetic effort. Love is personified as an officious man of letters far removed from the heroic poet of earlier ages. The poem, the I's final ironic defense against disillusion, also dismisses the *Love Songs* as simply one of countless

---

33. De Gourmont, *The Natural Philosophy of Love*, 40.

tributes to the torments of love. Elsewhere, however, Mina Loy is less deprecatory of her efforts; she writes to Van Vechten that the *Love Songs* are "THE best since Sappho."

III   *A Problematic Universe*   There are no excrescences on the
absolute, to which man may pin his faith.
—"Aphorisms on Futurism"

The retreat from despair signaled by the ironic defensiveness of the final love song is completed in four poems published between 1917 and 1920. To say that in these poems Mina Loy becomes an optimist is to simplify her acute understanding of the ambiguities and paradoxes of the human situation. Rather, she retreats to an existentialist engagement with cosmic chaos and mystery. In "Parturition" and the *Love Songs* she sought *the Answer* to the mystery; now she emphasizes the quest for that answer. Humanity, she knows, usually fails of its goal, but the Sisyphian struggle is self-justifying. "Human Cylinders," an examination of the failure of love and intellect to overcome human isolation, concludes with a warning against universe-destroying definitions:

> which of us
> Would not
> Receiving the holy-ghost
> Catch it   and caging
>   Lose it
> Or in the problematic
> Destroy the Universe
> With a solution.

This warning reappears in "The Black Virginity" (1918). The poem satirizes both the ignorant innocence that becomes a "black virginity" and religion's division of the world into black and white absolutes, absolutes symbolized by the black robes of novitiates for the priesthood and the white dresses of school girls. The novitiates have denied the potential of youth: "Fluted black silk cloaks / Hung square from shoulders / Truncated juvenility / Uniform segregation / Union in severity / Modulation / Intimida-

tion / Pride of misapprehended preparation / Ebony statues train-
ing for immobility." One of the novitiates in groping for a fruit in
the archetypal "Public Garden" enacts mankind's inevitable
failure to attain absolute knowledge: "The last with apostolic
lurch / Tries for a high hung fruit / And misses / Any way it is
inedible / It is always thus / In the Public Garden."

"The Dead" (1920) explores the inedible quality of such knowledge. Explaining that there are questions whose answers exceed
the understanding of the living, the dead conclude that "Only in
the segregated angles of Lunatic Asylums / Do those who have
strained to exceeding themselves / Break on our edgeless contours."

If the lunatic asylum and "black virginity" represent the de-
structiveness of absolutes, the sunlit abandon of the youth in "O
Hell" represents the alternative of unreflective freedom from
self-and-world definitions:

> Our person is a covered entrance to infinity
> Choked with the tatters of tradition
>
> Goddesses and Young Gods
> Caress the sanctity of Adolescence
> In the shaft of the sun.

But as the poem implies, such freedom is possible only for the
gods and the young. Mina Loy's mature narrator, recognizing
that the world and her own cerebral disposition will not long
permit such forgetfulness, creates a compromise. As the narrator of "The Black Virginity" she chooses to live in the sunlight;
there, all absolutes in abeyance, she strives through vigilant ob-
servation of life's shifting illusions to glimpse the absolute that
underlies them. A lilac print dress images her withdrawal from
black and white absolutes: "It is an old religion that put us in our
places / Here am I in lilac print / Preposterously no less than the
world flesh and devil / Having no more idea what those are /
What I am / Than Baby Priests of what "He" is / or they are."

CHAPTER THREE

"Radium of the Word"

Today is the crisis in consciousness.
　　　—"Aphorisms on Futurism"

"That was the time of James Joyce's *Ulysses* when the Word was made. The undisciplined word, seeking a new discipline, was prominent in everything she set her hand to."
　　　—William Carlos Williams, Preface to
　　　Lunar Baedeker & Time-Tables

I   The Objective

The structural and typographical experiments that shape the movement of consciousness in Mina Loy's poetry draw the reader's attention to the single word as meaning, shape, and sound. The word—in isolation, in unlikely conjunctions, or intertwined in glittering patterns of sound—is the sinew of her technical experiments and the pulse of her metaphysics and aesthetics. The emphasis on language derives in part from Loy's heritage in the Decadence, but more important it signifies her charter membership in the "generation of the word" which sought in the early twentieth century to rejuvenate the desiccated language of English and American poetry. She shares with her generation the sense of a "crisis in consciousness" and like them undertakes to restore to language honesty and vigor, clarity and exactness, and to make the movement of words correspond to (new) ways of seeing.[1] The word is the reagent of consciousness.

Mina Loy illustrates the function of the word as self-and-

---

1. Jerome Rothenberg (ed.), *Revolution of the Word: A Gathering of American Avant Garde Poetry 1914–1915* (New York: Seabury Press, 1974), xvi, discusses the "counterpoetics" of modernists like Mina Loy and Gertrude Stein that "presents . . . a fundamentally new view of the relationship between consciousness, language & poetic structure: what is seen, said & made."

world shaper in *Anglo-Mongrels and the Rose*, the semi-autobiographical poem that uses the child's awakening consciousness as a metaphor for the artist's interaction with the world.
The incipient selfhood of the child-heroine Ova is first imaged
as the eyes of the new-born baby: "Out of a fatted frown / this
spirit pokes its eyes / its star tipped handy-pandies / darting the
air." Grown to mobility, the baby craves what she sees: "The
suctional soul / clings to the vari—pinct universe." And "Her
entity / she projects / into these sudden colours / for self identification." But the objects of her delight—the fire, her father's
physic bottles—are inevitably withdrawn and her entity "is lost
in recurrent annihilation / with an old desperate unsurprise." Finally consciousness becomes articulate in words whose sounds
express her feelings:

> The child
>> whose wordless
>> thoughts
>> grow like visionary plants
>
>> finds
>> nothing objective new
>> and only words
>> mysterious
>
>> Sometimes a new word comes to her
>> she looks before her
>> and watches
>> for its materialization

Such a word is *diarrhea*, to the child's ear a lovely "iarrhea."
Hearing it, Ova's "cerebral / mush" swings to a spool of red
thread and to the pin worn by her mother,

>> And instantly
>> this fragmentary
>> simultaneity
>> of ideas
>
>> embodies
>>> the word

Ova is constructing an arbitrary word-world whose destruction by social and linguistic conventions threatens the artist in the soul of this Everychild. Fortunately, a child sometimes avoids "maturity" to become an artist and challenge clichéd patterns of thought and experience in order to give the self and the world back to us freed from the staleness of tradition. For Mina Loy, among poets the exemplary self and world liberator is Gertrude Stein, to whom she pays tribute in a two-part article that begins with this epigraph:

> Curie
> of the laboratory
> of vocabulary
>   she crushed
> the tonnage
> of consciousness
> congealed to phrases
>   to extract
> a radium of the word[2]

The poetic process imaged here is, paradoxically, one of simultaneous destruction and creation. Old phrases are exploded to liberate the word and its shaping energy. Loy explains the paradox by guiding the reader through the "grammatical lacunae" of several of Stein's seemingly chaotic images; for example, "This is the sun in. This is the lamb of the lantern of chalk." To see and create freshly as Stein requires, the imagination must shoot "for a fraction of a second through associated memories": "Of sun worship. Lamb worship. Lamb of, light of, the world. (Identical in christian symbolism.) Shepherd carries lantern. The lantern=lamb's eyes. Chalk white of lamb. Lantern sunshine in chalk pit=absolution of whiteness=pascal lamb=chalk easter toy for peasants." The associations may vary but the process is constructive: "The uncustomary impetus of her style ac-

2. Mina Loy, "Gertrude Stein," *Transatlantic Review*, II (1924), 305. Mike Weaver, *William Carlos Williams: The American Background* (Cambridge: Cambridge University Press, 1971), 214, cites this radium image as the source of the lines "a dissonance / in the valence of uranium" in *Paterson*.

celerates and extends the thought wave until it can vibrate a cosmos from a ray of light on a baa lamb." [3]

Joining Gertrude Stein in the forefront of verbal research was Mina Loy's mentor F. T. Marinetti. He revolted against linguistic tradition to create "words at liberty," words reborn in a process of destruction and distortion. By elimination of syntax and by the use of bizarre typographical arrangements, and by "cutting them [words] down and lengthening them, strengthening their centres or their extremities, augmenting or diminishing the number of their vowels and consonants," he hoped "to attain the *psycho-onomatopoeic chord*, sonorous yet abstract expression of an emotion or of pure thought." [4] The generation's awareness of the destruction/creation paradox is summarized by William Carlos Williams in an appreciation of the language of Marianne Moore: The reader "will perceive absolutely nothing except that his whole preconceived scheme of values has been ruined. And this is exactly what he should see, a break through all preconception of poetic form and mood and pace, a flaw, a crack in the bowl. It is this that one means when he says destruction and creation are simultaneous." [5] The paradox is true of the best of Mina Loy's poetry. In "The Costa San Giorgio" and the *Love Songs*, for example, the word destroys linear sequence and assumes the shifting configurations of life's flux and confusion. Elsewhere it shapes the self's fleeting intuitions of purpose in startling, compressed images that seem to the timid eye the destruction of form and value. The word violates verbal etiquette to express the reality of selfhood.

II   *The Method: Logopoeia*

Ezra Pound's early assessment of Mina Loy's poetry still offers a helpful introduction to her use of language. In Pound's view she

3. Loy, "Gertrude Stein," 430.
4. F. T. Marinetti, "Wireless Imagination and Words at Liberty," trans. Arundel del Re, *Poetry and Drama*, III (1913), 326.
5. William Carlos Williams, "Marianne Moore" (1931), in *Selected Essays of William Carlos Williams* (New York: New Directions, 1954), 121.

writes "logopoeia or poetry that is akin to nothing but language, which is a dance of the intelligence among words and ideas and modification of ideas and characters." He cites Jules Laforgue as the significant forerunner and singles out Marianne Moore (who adamantly denied Laforgue's influence) and T. S. Eliot as other practitioners of the mode; of course Pound might have included himself. He expands his definition by distinguishing logopoeia from "melopoeia," poetry significant for its music, and "imagism" (later labeled "phanopoeia"), poetry dependent on the image.[6] Certainly the image also is important in Loy's poetry, as is the music of her sound patterns. However, these qualities are secondary to what Pound calls logopoeia: a poetry of ideas and wordplay. In method it "employs words not only for their direct meaning, but it takes count in a special way of habits of usage, of the context we *expect* to find with the word, its usual concomitants, of its known acceptances, and of ironical play."[7]

Explications of Pound's definition and Laforgue's practice have stressed semantic "malleability," the use of extra-literary words and phrases outside their usual context, generally for irony.[8] In regard to Laforgue, a survey of his diction establishes five categories: scientific, religious, philosophical, and colloquial terms, as well as literary allusions.[9] These, one critic notes of Laforguian logopoeia in general, "produce an effect directly contrary to their effect in the usual contexts. Thus magniloquence can be deployed *against* magniloquence, vulgarity *against* vulgarity, and poeticisms *against* poeticizing."[10] For example, in the fol-

6. Ezra Pound "'Others,'" *Little Review*, IV (March, 1918), 57.

7. Ezra Pound, *How to Read* (London: Desmond Harmsworth, 1931), 25–26.

8. Semantic "malleability" comes from N. Christoph de Nagy, "The Place of Laforgue in Ezra Pound's Literary Criticism," in Warren Ramsey (ed.), *Jules Laforgue: Essays on a Poet's Life and Work* (Carbondale: Southern Illinois University Press, 1969), 111–29. Similar definitions are provided by J. P. Sullivan, *Ezra Pound and Sextus Propertius: A Study in Creative Translation* (Austin: University of Texas Press, 1964), 64–76; and David Perkins, *A History of Modern Poetry: From the 1890s to the High Modernist Mode* (Cambridge: Harvard University Press, 1976), 471–72.

9. François Ruchon, *Jules Laforgue, sa Vie, son Oeuvre* (Geneva: 1924), 161, cited in de Nagy, "The Place of Laforgue in Ezra Pound's Literary Criticism," 125.

10. Sullivan, *Ezra Pound and Sextus Propertius*, 67.

lowing lines from Laforgue's "Preludes Autobiographiques" the medical term "hypertrophique" jars against the melancholy tone and mocks the speaker's sense of himself as a scientific oddity. Furthermore, the probable allusion in the first line to Petrarch's Laura sonnet XXXV contrasts a genuinely suffering lover to Laforgue's ironic misogynist; the rapid, ironic deflation is characteristic of Laforgue:

> Seul, pur, songeur,
> Me croyant hypertrophique! comme un plongeur
> Aux mouvants bosquets des savanes sous-marines,
> J'avais roulé par les livres, bon misogyne.[11]

Mina Loy employs a Laforguian vocabulary and imagery to similar ends. We have seen in the *Love Songs* how romantic love deflates to "mucous membrane," "saliva," the phallic "skin-sack," and "spermatozoa." In "The Effectual Marriage," one of the poems that prompted Pound's label, "sialagogues" (a term meaning agents that stimulate the flow of saliva) seems inappropriately erudite among the domestic commonplaces of the kitchen. Gina, wife of the scholarly Miovanni, looks out her kitchen window,

> From among his pots and pans
> Where he so kindly kept her
> Where she so wisely busied herself
> Pots and Pans   she cooked in them
> All sorts of sialagogues
> Some say   that happy women are immaterial

"Sialagogues" is, however, more than felicitous wordplay; it participates in the "dance of the intelligence" that is logopoeia. "Sialagogues" resolves the uneasy tension created by the nuances of "kindly" and "wisely," confirming the suspicion that all is not bliss in this house. It does so because it is an abstraction

11. Jules Laforgue, "Preludes Autobiographiques," *Oeuvres Poétiques*, ed. Hubert Juin (Paris: Éditions Pierre Belfond, 1965), 29. "Alone, pure, pensive, / Believing myself hypertrophic! like a diver / Among the moving thickets of underwater savannahs, / I have been tossed by the books, a good misogynist."

(the sort of term Miovanni might use) that makes woman's work and, hence, woman herself "immaterial" as regards the worldly concerns of men.

Mina Loy also shares Laforgue's colloquial tone, verging on ennui and despair, and his preference for polysyllabic words. These qualities are reflected in the description of Gina as a woman who wanted

> To be everything in woman
> Everything everyway at once
> Diurnally variegate
> Miovanni always knew her
> She was Gina
> Gina who lent monogamy
> With her fluctuant aspirations
> A changeant consistency
> Unexpected intangibilities.

The polysyllables embody the difficulty of expressing the ambiguities of Gina's selfhood, a selfhood Miovanni matter-of-factly reduces to "She was Gina."

In placing Mina Loy's poems among the generation's Laforguian experiments with the word, we might note the polysyllabic streets of *Prufrock*—"Streets that follow like a tedious argument / Of insidious intent," and Mauberley's alienation from his age—"Mildness, amid the neo-Nietzschean clatter, / His sense of graduations, / Quite out of place amid / Resistance to current exacerbations." These ponderous, self-mocking abstractions that reflect a Decadent ennui differ considerably from the conscientious detailing of particulars characteristic of Marianne Moore's verbalism. In her contributions to the *Others* anthology for 1917 she also employs polysyllabic abstractions, but a complex syntax and syllabic meter give her poetry a restraint uncommon in the works of other writers of logopoeia. Take, for example, "My Apish Cousins" ("The Monkeys"):

> It is not for all of us to understand art—
>   finding it

> All so difficult, examining the thing
>
> As if it were something inconceivably arcanic, as
> Symmetrically frigid as something carved out of
> chrysoprase
> Or marble—

Pound's linking of Marianne Moore and Mina Loy can be accounted for by their shared complexity of diction and their commitment to a poetry of ideas; he notes the "arid clarity . . . of le tempérament de l'Americaine" and characterizes them as poets more of the head than the heart.[12] Both women were fascinated by words and challenged the reader to a strenuous navigation of their verbal labyrinths. In the age of Imagism both persevered in singular combinations of idea and image. But whereas the "observations" of Marianne Moore move from precise descriptions of objects, people, and animals to considered moral and ethical judgments, Mina Loy's verbal flourishes, contained in straightforward syntax rather than Moore's convoluted sentences, yield social and self satire and cosmic analysis.

An integral part of logopoeia in Loy's poetry is the emphasis of sound patterns, often combined with an exotic diction, that she and a few of her contemporaries adopted from Laforgue and the English Decadents. Carried to extremes, such a practice becomes verbal decor and is readily combined with the posturings of the dandy. In America the manner throve among contributors to *Rogue*, especially Walter Conrad Arensberg, Donald Evans, and Wallace Stevens.[13] One of the *Rogue* group in absentia, Mina Loy throughout her poetry practiced a roguish verbalism that is the trademark of her poetry and often its strength, as poet Denise Levertov notes: "An appetite for sounds—for words as sounds—which results in a scintillating precision. And it's this

---

12. Pound, " 'Others,'" 58.
13. Robert Buttel, *Wallace Stevens: The Making of Harmonium* (Princeton: Princeton University Press, 1967), 80–101; Kenneth Fields, "Past Masters: Walter Conrad Arensberg and Donald Evans," *Southern Review*, n.s. VI (1970), 317–39.

that makes for—IS—the close reasoning: it's there IN the words! Here's a virtue! There in words, which are sounds, which once were made up experimentally by our forebears—don't we live in a daily forgetting of that?" [14]

Mina Loy consistently employs sound patterning in both her abstract analyses and her compressed, vivid images. Sound provides emphasis and replaces the rigid formal and moral control of metric as a means of unifying line, image, stanza, and poem. [15] Poem xxvi of the *Love Songs*, for example, mimics in shiftings of sound the mincing secretiveness of the clownish lovers:

> Shedding our petty pruderies
> From slit eyes
>
> We sidle up
> To Nature
> ——— that irate pornographist

The consonants *s*, *d*, and *p* dominate the opening line, *s-d* of *shedding* becoming the *d-s* of *pruderies*. The *d* and its fellow alveolar stop *t*, as well as the plosive stop *p*, slow the line to imitate the furtive hesitations of the lovers. In the second line, *from* introduces the *f-m* pattern, but maintains continuity by inverting the *o-r* of *our*. *S* and *t* are also repeated, but the *l* of *slit* precipitates a new configuration in *sidle* of the third line (one could say that the sounds of the poem are involved in a "sidling" action). *Up* faintly echoes the *p*'s of the first line. *To Nature*, naming the cosmic immovable object obstructing the lovers, is isolated by typography (the line has been gradually shortened in length and number of syllables) and by sound. While the line

14. Denise Levertov, "Notes of Discovery," in Preface to *Lunar Baedeker & Time-Tables: Selected Poems of Mina Loy* (Highlands, N.C.: Jonathan Williams, 1958). Linda W. Wagner, *Denise Levertov* (New York: Twayne, 1967), Chapter 4, in examining Levertov's careful attention to sound, suggests the reason for her praise of Mina Loy.

15. David Antin, "Modernism and Postmodernism: Approaching the Present in American Poetry," *Boundary 2*, I (1972), 116–18, discusses the moral implications of the modernist use of metric.

introduces the *o*, *n*, *a* and -*ture* sounds, the *t* provides continuity. The resolution of the poem's image and idea in the final line is accompanied by a tying together of the sound patterns. The *a* of *nature* appropriately reappears three times in the appositive personification, while the *p* of *pornographist* links the final word to the image *petty pruderies*. The *i* of *irate* concludes the prominent *i* of *eyes* and *sidle*; the *t* concludes *petty*, *slit*, and *to*. In *pornographist* the *ro* of *from* reverts to its original *o-r* pattern in *our*, while the *ph* recalls *from*, and *ist* repeats the opening *s*. However the forceful, simpering *s* of the first line has given way to an abrasive *r* appropriate to the irony of the final line. The fact that *we* of the third line finds no echoing sound pattern emphasizes the isolation of the lovers in the indifferent cosmic scheme of things.

By such careful attention to sound Mina Loy delineates her verbal images with the hard edges I have previously compared to the sharply etched contours of Surrealist painting. Remember the opening lines of the *Love Songs*:

> Spawn   of   Fantasies
> Silting the appraisable
> Pig Cupid   his rosy snout
> Rooting erotic garbage

In part the hard-edged quality derives from the concrete and specific diction. "Spawn," "Silting," "Pig Cupid," "rosy snout," "Rooting," "garbage"—all conjure up specific objects or actions, while "Fantasies," "appraisable," and "erotic" are abstractions. Hardness of image is also obtained by a compression that juxtaposes words from different categories of diction: the biological and psychological ("Spawn"/"Fantasies," "Silting"/"appraisable"); the bestial and romantic ("Pig Cupid," "rosy snout," "erotic garbage"). Loy eliminates all but the key words, often to the point of verbal collage, although she stops short of Marinetti's "words at liberty." Underlying the concreteness and compression, an intricate pattern of sound unifies lines and images while at the same time sharply distinguishing words from each other. The pattern of stops in "Pig Cupid" exemplifies such sound-sharpness as does the variation of initial word sounds.

Sound as a unifying device is often used more subtly, as in the opening stanza of "July in Vallombrosa" where it creates the hushed ambient of a sanatorium:

> Old lady sitting still
> Pine trees standing quite still
> Sister of mercy   whispering
> Oust the Dryad

Sometimes sound is obtrusively satiric. In "Apology of Genius" (1922), for instance, it expresses the alienated artists' view of their public: "smooth fool's faces / like buttocks bared in aboriginal mockeries." It may also make puns, as in *Anglo-Mongrels* where the guests at a literary tea are described as "wiseacres and waisted-women." And sound frequently applies the cutting edge to satiric abstractions. In "The Effectual Marriage" sound interplays emphasize the evasive ambiguities of the marriage and the elusive reality of Gina. In *Anglo-Mongrels* they suggest the rigid and grating propriety of British pressures to conformity. The *r* is harsh, the *i* an irritating pin prick to conscience, the plosive *p* and *b* shows of force, and the *t* a diligently honed barb of restraint:

> Rose of arrested impulses
> self pruned
> of the primordial attributes
> —A tepid heart   inhibiting
> with tactful terrorism
> the (Blossom) Populous
> to mystic incest with its ancestry

Finally, sound patterning is often combined with distinctive typographical arrangements. A passage in *Anglo-Mongrels* describing the movement of Ova's eye epitomizes Loy's use of typography to emphasize the word as theme (consciousness), line, and sound:

A
lucent
iris
shifts
its
irradiate
interstice

glooms and relumes
on an orb of verdigris

III   "Lunar Baedeker"

Lunar Baedeker (1923) contains the maturation of Mina Loy's experiments with the word and gives good indication that she is keeping pace with contemporary researchers in the "laboratory / of vocabulary." She has not written as much as some, but her work has been as adventuresome and often as accomplished as that of the future modernist giants who, circa 1923, were also publishing significant early volumes. For instance, 1923 saw the publication of Wallace Stevens' *Harmonium*, William Carlos Williams' *Spring and All*, and Ernest Hemingway's *In Our Time*; Marianne Moore's *Observations* appeared in 1924. Like the works of Williams and Hemingway (and in 1925 *The Making of Americans* by Gertrude Stein), *Lunar Baedeker* was published in Dijon, France, by Robert McAlmon, the American expatriate writer and publisher who gave generous and unpretentious assistance to many aspiring modernists. In the case of Mina Loy, one of McAlmon's special friends, the little volume he made possible remains the most important tribute from her contemporaries. It contains eleven "Poems 1921–1922" and eight "Poems 1914–1915."

In the 1921–1922 section language is the implicit, sometimes explicit, subject. In four poems on individual artists Loy per-

forms the tour de force of creating in her own medium—words
—the essence of admired artists and gives her most finely craft-
ed demonstration of the word as shaper. The word shapes the
voluptuous simplicity of Constantin Brancusi's *Golden Bird*, the
trenchant wit of James Joyce's *Ulysses*, the chill beauty of Edgar
Allen Poe's death chambers, and the cerebral austerity of Wyndham Lewis' *The Starry Sky*, just as the metal, words, and paint of
these artists shape the world.

To evoke the glistening brass simplicity of Brancusi's abstraction of flight Mina Loy causes her words to glide on a subdued
and scintillating *s* from the soft glottal *c* to the liquid *l* and rolling
r: "an incandescent curve / licked by chromatic flames / in labyrinths of reflections." The verbal wizardry of Joyce, whom she
invokes as "Master / of meteoric idiom," she depicts in liquid *l*'s
and sibilant *s*'s that culminate in an epigram of the human condition dominated by forceful *sp*, *f*, and *t* sounds:

> The loquent consciousness
> of living things
> pours in torrential languages
>
> The elderly colloquists
> the Spirit and the Flesh
> are out of tongue — — —

In "Poe" (1921) elegant diction combined with liquid *l*'s and
slow, cool vowels evokes an exotic death chamber:

> a lyric elixir of death
>
> embalms
> the spindle spirits of your hour glass loves
> on moon spun nights

In "'The Starry Sky' of Wyndham Lewis" words emulate the in-
terlocking Cubist blocks of Lewis' painting in abstract diction
and irregular line length:

> who raised
> these rocks of human mist

> pyramidical survivors
> in the cyclorama of space
>
> in the
> austere theatre of the Infinite
>   the ghosts of the stars
> perform the "Presence"

All the later poems of *Lunar Baedeker* are, like the artist poems, implicitly about the self-analytical power of words. Mina Loy's reliance on sound patterns emphasizes this quality inherent in good poetry. Her most extravagant effort at self-analytical language is the title poem "Lunar Baedeker." A satire of moon-struck escapists (Decadents, dandies, idealist-reformers) who have fled the responsibilities of clear, sunlit vision, the poem re-creates their exotic lunar refuge in a decor of Decadence shaped by gilded words and images, and lush patterns of sound. The satire derives first from the excessive opulence of diction and sound, and second from the motif of death woven into the lunar landscape by words like *posthumous*, *infusoria* (organisms found in decaying matter like bone phosphorous), *tombstones*, *dooms-day*, *Necropolis*, *mildews*, and *fossil*. The exotic vocabulary of escape becomes a tomb.

"Lunar Baedeker" is also important for the evolution of the image-stanza it represents. The alternation of abstraction and image, such as in "Parturition" and "The Effectual Marriage," is replaced by vivid images that unite the two aspects of consciousness—intellect and intuition—in instants of penetrating vision. Loy has previously used such abstract-concrete images, but rarely in the rapid succession of this poem. Although syntactically related, these images, as in a collage, are juxtaposed and connected more by the mind's associations than by sequential logic: they could be rearranged with little alteration of idea. Of course this image sequence can be understood as an implementation of the Futurist-Bergsonian admonition that the poem should be an uninterrupted sequence of images. The poem uses the iambic foot, but short, irregular lines diminish the unifying effect of the iamb except as it sometimes helps to emphasize a single line or image. Image and sound have replaced meter and rhyme as the controlling devices, and the most pronounced rhythm exists in the movement from image to image. Most of the image-stanzas are built around the verb—isolated in a single line or emphatically positioned at the end of a line.[16] The hard-edged quality that proceeds from the precise, compressed, sound-sensitive diction prompted Yvor Winters to describe the result as "images that have frozen into epigrams."[17]

> A silver Lucifer
> serves
> cocaine in cornucopia
>
> To some somnambulists
> of adolescent thighs
> draped
> in satirical draperies
>
> Peris in livery
> prepare
> Lethe
> for posthumous parvenues
>
> Delirious Avenues
> lit
> with the chandelier souls
> of infusoria
> from Pharaoh's tombstones

16. Kenneth Fields, "The Rhetoric of Artifice—Ezra Pound, T. S. Eliot, Wallace Stevens, Walter Conrad Arensberg, Donald Evans, Mina Loy and Yvor Winters" (Ph.D. dissertation, Stanford University, 1967), 215–16, discusses her "rhythmic deficiency." Fields examines Loy's debt to the Parnassian emphasis on style, finding her less accomplished than her contemporaries in the perfection of style, and discusses her effort to combine style and an exploration of ideas.

17. Yvor Winters, "Mina Loy," Dial, LXXX (1926), 498.

lead
to mercurial doomsdays
Odious oasis
in furrowed phosphorous — — —

the eye-white sky-light
white-light district
of lunar lusts

— — — Stellectric signs
"Wing shows on Starway"
"Zodiac carrousel"

Cyclones
of ecstatic dust
and ashes whirl
crusaders
from hallucinatory citadels
of shattered glass
into evacuate craters

A flock of dreams
browse on Necropolis

From the shores
of oval oceans
in the oxidised Orient

Onyx-eyed Odalisques
and ornithologists
observe
the flight
of Eros obsolete

And "Immortality"
mildews
in the museums of the moon

"Nocturnal cyclops"
"Crystal concubine"
— — — — — —

Pocked with personification
the fossil virgin of the skies
waxes and wanes — — — —

Laforgue's considerable influence upon Mina Loy finds further substantiation in the borrowings of "Lunar Baedeker" from "Climat, Faune et Flore de la Lune" and the other lunar devotions of *L'Imitation de Notre-Dame la Lune*. As the following stanza from "Climat . . ." demonstrates, Mina Loy adopts Laforgue's Decadent language and imagery for their shared purpose of criticizing the flight from reality:

> Oui, c'est l'automne incantatoire et permanent
> Sans thermomètre, embaumant mers et continents,
> Etangs aveugles, lac ophtalmiques, fontaines
> De Léthé, cendres d'air, déserts de porcelaine,
> Oasis, solfatares, cratères éteints,
> Arctiques sierras, cataractes l'air en zinc,
> Hauts-plateaux crayeux, carrières abandonnées,
> Nécropoles moins vieilles que leurs graminées,
> Et des dolmens par caravanes,—et tout très
> Ravi d'avoir fait son temps, de rêver au frais.[18]

Laforgue's presence is felt especially in the final image of "Lunar Baedeker." This personification of the moon as a pocked, fossil virgin resembles several images by Laforgue that, as his translator Patricia Terry says, reproach "our false humanizing of the cosmos."[19] The clipped, epigrammatic style also suggests itself as a model for Loy's image-stanzas:

> Astre fossile
> Que tout exile
> —"Litanies des Premiers Quartiers de la Lune"
>
> Et la lune a, bonne vieille,

18. Jules Laforgue, "Climat, Faune et Flore de la Lune," *Oeuvres Poétiques*, 167: "Yes, it is the magical and permanent autumn / Without thermometer, embalming seas and continents, / Blind pools, ophthalmic lakes, fountains / Of lethe, ashes of the air, deserts of porcelain, / Oases, sulphur springs, extinct craters, / Arctic sierras, zinc cataracts, / Chalky high plateaus, abandoned quarries, / Necropolises less old than their graminaceae, / And dolmen in caravans—and all very / Happy to have done their duty, to dream in the cool wind."

19. Patricia Terry (trans.), Introduction, *Poems of Jules Laforgue* (Berkeley: University of California Press, 1958), 11.

Du coton dans les oreilles.
—"Complainte de la Lune en Province"[20]

IV   *Later Poetry*

The Laforguian parallel returns us to the logopoeia, the "dance of the intelligence" said by Pound to define the poetry of Mina Loy. Clearly, what weighs equally with her dedication to "the word" is her commitment to ideas: verbal experiment is checked by the desire to communicate. Hence Mina Loy does not employ the word arbitrarily, as does her child-persona Ova, or liberate it to the radical fragmentations of Gertrude Stein or Marinetti. Instead she modifies their techniques to invigorate, but not obfuscate, her analyses of aspiration, ignorance, and blindness. Her poetry is often abstract and didactic, aspects of her Victorian heritage against which she did not revolt in practice, although as we shall see in the next chapter against which she did argue. Concerned in some of her most innovative poetry with the movement of consciousness, she more typically analyzes an individual within a situation that illuminates her metaphysics. By this discursive method she separates herself from the Imagists, writers of phanopoeia. She demonstrates her awareness of the contribution made to a vital poetry by concrete, specific imagery, but even her most vivid imagery usually contains abstractions. Whereas the Imagist poem tends to be a brief metaphor or description presenting one object or feeling "in an instant of time," the poems of Mina Loy are extended analyses of the human condition. Sound interplays provide unity and emphasis as they choreograph the dance of the intelligence within line, image, and poem.

This penchant for ideas and abstractions is nicely expressed in

20. Laforgue, "Litanies des Premiers Quartiers de la Lune" and "Complainte de la Lune en Province," *Oeuvres Poétiques*, 161, 66: "Fossil star / Exiled by everything"; "And the Moon, a good old lady / With cotton in her ears."

the image of the "cerebral forager," from the *Love Songs*: "Green things grow / Salads / For the cerebral / Forager's revival." This abstract/concrete image reflects the aesthetic balance Mina Loy found in images of concrete reality and her need to balance intellectuality with Futurist dynamism or peasant unreflectiveness. But in spite of the dangers cerebralness posed for selfhood and poetry she exploited it for her public image. It comes through in her letters to Van Vechten and her article on Gertrude Stein; and Robert McAlmon and Alfred Kreymborg remembered the cerebral quality of her conversation.[21] It is especially evident in this comment to a newspaper interviewer: "If you are very frank with yourself and don't mind how ridiculous anything that comes to you may seem, you will have a chance of capturing the symbol of your direct reaction."[22] If we accept Mina Loy's definition of modern art, this cerebralness, combined with sound interplays and exotic diction, is the map by which the reader might discover her authorship. She says in her unpublished "The Metaphysical Pattern in Aesthetics" that the modern artist is known by his distinctive manipulation of the medium, not by his subject matter:

> The pattern of a work of art is interposed between the artist's creation and the observer in the mode of a screen formed by the directing lines or map of the artist's genius.
>
> This is the essential factor in a work of art.
>
> The old masters presented the esoteric plan of their individuality superimposed upon a "subject."

21. Alfred Kreymborg, *Troubadour: An Autobiography* (New York: Boni and Liveright, 1925), 170, recalls the "redoubtable Mina Loy" among the *Rogue* crowd where he was "sure that the indirect method of speech adapted by each person present betrayed an aesthetic fastidiousness in the matter of living as well as of expressing art." Robert McAlmon, *Being Geniuses Together, 1920–1930*, ed. Kay Boyle (Garden City, N.Y.: Doubleday, 1968), 41, compares the "brilliant" conversation of Mina Loy and Jane Heap: "Mina, her cerebral fantasies, Jane, her breezy, traveling-salesman-of-the-world tosh which was impossible to recall later. But neither of these ladies needed to make sense. Conversation is an art with them, something entirely unrelated to sense or reality or logic."

22. "Do You Strive to Capture the Symbols of Your Reactions? If Not You Are Quite Old Fashioned," New York *Evening Sun*, February 13, 1917, p. 10.

The moderns present the map of their individuality without the secondary reconstruction of the pictorial coherence of our customary vision.

Every time we recognise the work of any given master it is by the singularity of this map of his aesthetic system. Never by the subject.[23]

The map of Mina Loy's later work is distinguished from the earlier only by the diminished luster of the diction. "Ephemerid" (1944/1946) alternates description of a child's make-believe game with a meditation on fantasy. The opening sets the discursive context: "The Eternal is sustained by serial metamorphosis, / even so Beauty is // metamorphosis surprises!" The child, dressed in an old curtain, is then described as "a magnified imago": "some aerial, unbeknown / eerie-form / of dual mobility, / / having long wing, an unbelievable / imp-fly." These images interweave the concrete and abstract, but the poem yields to abstraction:

> towing in twofold progress
> nameless nostalgia through slush,
> enigma along gloom.
>
> As always, has a wisp of whiteness loveliness
> to lift the eyelids;
> to whisper of subvisual resources
> in the uncolor of the unknown.

The Laforguian attraction to exotic, scientific, and polysyllabic words continues; and sound effectively unifies the passage, especially in the second stanza above where the *w*, *s*, *l*, and *i* sounds trace the delicate, ephemeral beauty of childhood fantasy.

"Hilarious Israel" (1947), the presentation of a Jewish show-

23. Mina Loy, "The Metaphysical Pattern in Aesthetics" (Typescript in Collection of American Literature, Beinecke Rare Book and Manuscript Library, Yale University).

man who has substituted Broadway for the Wailing Wall, combines the abstract and concrete in a pattern of muted sound:

> History inclines to you
> as a dental surgeon
> over the sufferer's chair
>
> has self-sought anaesthesia
> dazed you
> into theatrical lairs?

The imagery is not as brilliant as a "Pig Cupid" or a "silver Lucifer"; the passionate revolt and acerbic satire that fired the early poetry have cooled to quiet meditations on human accommodations to cosmic indifference. While the simile is original and concrete, it lacks Loy's characteristic compression and the diction itself is unexceptional. A more serious falling off in vitality appears in "Faun Fare" (1962), a satire of the sexual ambiguity of the guests at a cocktail party. We have only to remember the "silver Lucifer" who "serves / cocaine in cornucopia" to remark the lessened intensity of diction and vision. The sound interplays are formulaic; the fresh, sometimes shocking word is replaced by a gimmicky prefix:

> Surreptitious fanfare
> of unadams
> amingle with ouradams
>
> a seemingly uniform guesthood
> met in unsolemn sociability

But the comparison also reminds us of Loy's accomplishments with the radiant "Word." And her persistent effort to focus the reader's attention on language reminds us of her commitment to the rejuvenation of language. A remark to Van Vechten (July, 1915) reflects her lifelong objective to speak honestly of experience, and it singles out perhaps her most important contribution to the ongoing research in the "laboratory / of vocabulary." Addressing the relative health of English and American poetry, she identifies herself with the Americans and then says, "I don't believe the men in England have got any of the new consciousness about things that is beginning to formulate in some of us—they cannot evaluate a reaction to any stimulus except through juggling with standard poetical phrases—if only they would realise that art always begins with a man's being quite simply honest with himself."

CHAPTER FOUR
Polarities of Vision

Lunar Baedeker introduces two emblematic figures who dominate the remainder of Mina Loy's poetry and complete the metaphysical scheme outlined in the poems of female selfhood. Vision remains the major theme, the eye the major motif and symbol. The first of these figures is the artist. He alone among humanity possesses the vision for intuiting the essence of life's chaos and the skill to shape his intuitions into form—the divine principle. The second figure is the bum, emblem of timid or failed vision, who seeks transcendence of worldly care in false Elysiums and Nirvanas. Both bum and artist strive to transcend chaos, but the bum has chosen a corrupt means. Together they establish the boundaries of human possibility. Exploring these boundaries in *Lunar Baedeker*, Mina Loy formulates her aesthetic, plants her modernist departures in nineteenth-century views of the artist and the art object, and introduces the subjects of her later poetry.

I   *The Artist*   In the raw caverns of the Increate
we forge the dusk of Chaos
to that imperious jewelry of the Universe
—the Beautiful—
—"Apology of Genius"

The aesthetic that shaped *Lunar Baedeker* continued the French tradition stretching from Théophile Gautier and art for art's sake through the Parnassians and Baudelaire to Symbolism and the English 1890s. Originating in the artist's alienation from the philistinism of society and his sense of social ineffectiveness, the tradition prized technical perfection and admired beauty severed from utilitarian and didactic ends. Mina Loy, like other moderns, draws selectively on the tradition in her revolt against Victorian art and mores. She adopts its contempt for middle-class values and its argument for the autonomy of art. Her concern with the rejuvenation of language can be traced to the art-for-art's-sake emphasis on form and style, that is to its attention to the craft of poetry. She also reflects the art-for-art's-sake advocacy of freedom of subject and its preference for the man-made subject, especially art objects and the city, over nature.[1] In *Lunar Baedeker* "Apology of Genius" acknowledges this heritage. In imagery, tone, and subject the poem resembles "Lunar Baedeker" except that, sympathetic to the alienated artist, it attacks the ignorant public that persecutes him:

> Ostracized as we are with God—
> > The watchers of the civilized wastes
> > reverse their signals on our track
>
> > Lepers of the moon
> > all magically diseased
> > we come among you
> > innocent
> > of our luminous sores
>
> > unknowing
> > how perturbing lights
> > our spirit
> > on the passion of Man
> > until you turn on us your smooth fool's faces
> > like buttocks bared in aboriginal mockeries
>
> > We are the sacerdotal clowns
> > who feed upon the wind and stars
> > and pulverous pastures of poverty

1. Helpful discussions of the various currents of art for art's sake appear in Robert Denommé, *The French Parnassian Poets* (Carbondale: Southern Illinois University Press, 1972); David Perkins, *A History of Modern Poetry: From the 1890s to the High Modernist Mode* (Cambridge: Harvard University Press, 1976), Chapter 3; and Enid Starkie, *From Gautier to Eliot: The Influence of France on English Literature, 1851–1939* (London: Hutchinson, 1960).

Our wills are formed
by curious disciplines
beyond your laws

You may give birth to us
or marry us
the chances of your flesh
are not our destiny—

The cuirass of the soul
still shines—
And we are unaware
if you confuse
such brief
corrosion with possession

In the raw caverns of the Increate
we forge the dusk of Chaos
to that imperious jewelry of the Universe
    —the Beautiful—

While to your eyes
    A delicate crop
of criminal mystic immortels
stands to the censor's scythe.

The opening association of artists with God introduces the theme of the artist's divine vocation and places the poem in direct line of descent from Baudelaire's "Bénédiction." The line "Ostracized as we are with God" paraphrases much of Baudelaire's poem, especially the first stanza:

Lorsque, par un décret des puissances suprêmes,
Le Poète apparaît en ce monde ennuyé,
Sa mère épouvantée et pleine de blasphèmes
Crispe ses poings vers Dieu, qui la prend en pitié[2]

2. Charles Baudelaire, "Bénédiction," *Les Fleurs du Mal*, ed. Antoine Adam (Paris: Éditions Garnier Frères, 1961), 9: "When, by a decree of the supreme powers, / The Poet appears in this tiresome world, / His mother, frightened and full of blasphemies, / Clenches her fists toward God, who takes pity on her."

Mina Loy's artists also seem under special dispensation from God, but the ambiguous "with" of the first line suggests that they are ostracized *from* God and may be descendants of Laforgue's "Pierrots (I)": "Ils sont de la secte du Blême, / Ils n'ont rien à voir avec Dieu."[3] A resolution lies in the double vision that operates throughout the poem. To the public the artist is ostracized *from* God, whereas the artist sees his own divinity and, as in "Bénédiction," finds his earthly sojourn a painful separation from celestial glory.[4] The public ("watchers of the civilized wastes"), like the belligerent public of "Bénédiction" who "s'accusent d'avoir mis leurs pieds dans ses pas,"[5] flee the artist— they "reverse their signals on our track."

The remainder of the poem images the artist's uniqueness and persecution. For the image of the artist as a martyr-clown Mina Loy is again indebted to Baudelaire and Laforgue. "Lepers of the moon," the public's hostile epithet, recalls Laforgue's pierrots with "La coeur blanc tatoué / De sentences lunaires." For the public the lunar image signifies a lunatic divorce from reality. But for the pierrot and the abused artist the moon represents alienation and revolt; it is a source of inspiration and an image "for sterility, for evasion by suicide, for unrealizable Romantic aspiration."[6] Like the lunar image the reference to the special food of the artist, in the fourth stanza, originates in Laforgue's "Pierrots (I)":

3. Jules Laforgue, "Pierrots (I)," *Oeuvres Poétiques*, ed. Hubert Juin (Paris: Éditions Pierre Belfond, 1965), 172: "They belong to the pale secte, / They have nothing to do with God."

4. Kenneth Fields, "The Poetry of Mina Loy," *Southern Review*, n.s. III (1967), 603, interprets "Lepers of the Moon" and "sacerdotal clowns" as "the public view of the artist."

5. Baudelaire, "Bénédiction," *Les Fleurs du Mal*, 10: "they accuse themselves of having followed in his footsteps."

6. Laforgue, "Pierrots (II)," *Oeuvres Poétiques*, 173: "The white heart tattooed, / With lunar maxims." Warren Ramsey, *Jules Laforgue and the Ironic Inheritance* (New York: Oxford University Press, 1953), 140, discusses various interpretations of the moon in Laforgue's *L'Imitation de Notre-Dame la Lune*, the precursor of Mina Loy's lunar poems.

> Ils vont, se sustentant d'azur!
> Et parfois aussi de légumes,
> De riz plus blanc que leur costume,
> De mandarines et d'oeufs durs.[7]

There are also resemblances to "Bénédiction," whose young artist takes his nourishment from nature: "Et dans tout ce qu'il boit et dans tout ce qu'il mange / Retrouve l'ambroisie et le nectar vermeil." Baudelaire's artist likewise sets the pattern for finding companionship in nature: "Il joue avec le vent, cause avec le nuage."[8]

In "Apology of Genius" such images of the artist's uniqueness are followed by images of the incompatibility of artist and public; then in the penultimate stanza the image of the artist as a blacksmith-God, forging Beauty from universal chaos, paraphrases the art-for-art's-sake aesthetic. Art, as "imperious jewelry" implies, is other than and superior to nature. The apotheosis of the artist and his creation is followed by another ironic image of the artist's victimization. The public dismisses artistic claimants to divinity as "criminal mystic immortels," flowers (*immortelles*) from Laforgue's Decadent garden whose improprieties doom them to the censor's vengeance. However, the public seems not to know that the *immortelle* is an everlasting flower which will withstand ostracism and censorship.

The rare commentators on Mina Loy's poetry generally concur that "Apology of Genius" is one of her best poems. Its excellence lies in the fact that, as Loy said of Gertrude Stein's work, it is "sufficiently satisfying as verbal design."[9] As in most of her poems Loy employs sound for satire and to enhance the lucid

7. Laforgue, "Pierrots (I)," *Oeuvres Poétiques*, 172: "They go, nourishing themselves on the sky! / And sometimes on vegetables also, / On rice whiter than their costume, / On mandarines and hard-boiled eggs."

8. Baudelaire, "Bénédiction," *Les Fleurs du Mal*, 9: "And in all that he drinks and in all that he eats / He finds sweet ambrosia and vermilion nectar"; "He plays with the wind, chats with the cloud."

9. Fields, "The Poetry of Mina Loy," 602–605. H[arriet] M[onroe], "Guide to the Moon," XXIII (1923), 100–103, reprinted the poem and added punctuation;

images of artistic uniqueness and persecution. "Lepers of the moon," "cuirass of the soul," and "criminal mystic immortels" are intricate patterns of sound and vivid epigrams shaped by an exotic, abstract/concrete diction. "Buttocks bared in aboriginal mockeries" jars the sonorities and liquid currents of the other images, its forceful plosives aping the vulgarity of the public's intolerance.

The contemptuous tone of *épater les bourgeoise*[10] that runs throughout the poem was adopted from art for art's sake as part of Loy's modernist stance. The tone becomes the substance of the manifesto-like "IN . . . Formation," a defense of the Independents Exhibition (1917). The piece combines art-for-art's-sake elitism and Dada's view of art as a game or joke. As in "Apology of Genius" the antagonism between artist and public derives from differences in vision:

> I do not suppose the Independents "will educate the public"—the only trouble with the public is education.
> *The Artist* is uneducated, is seeing IT for the first time; he can never see the same thing twice.
> Education is the putting of spectacles on wholesome eyes. The public does not naturally care about these spectacles, the cause of its quarrels with art. *The Public* likes to be jolly; *The Artist* is jolly and quite irresponsible. Art is *The Divine Joke*, and any *Public*, and any *Artist* can see a nice, easy, simple joke, such as the sun; but only artists and serious critics can look at a grayish stickiness on smooth canvas. . . . So *The Public* and *The Artist* can meet at every point except the—for *The Artist*—vital one, that of pure uneducated *seeing*. They like the same drinks, can fight in the same trenches, pretend to the same women; but never see the same thing ONCE.[11]

Sympathetic to the art-for-art's-sake defense of the artist, Mina Loy nevertheless condemns the escapist life-style and art

---

Yvor Winters and Kenneth Fields (eds.), *Quest for Reality: An Anthology of Short Poems in English* (Chicago: Swallow Press, 1969), complimented the poem by reprinting it. Mina Loy, "Gertrude Stein," *Transatlantic Review*, II (1924), 427.

10. Monroe, "Guide to the Moon," 101.

11. Mina Loy, "IN . . . Formation," *Blind Man*, No. 1 (April 10, 1917), 7.

of the Decadents and dandies who, at the end of the tradition have clownishly debased themselves and art. In *Lunar Baedeker* these escapists provide a contrast for the heroic artists who dedicatedly strive for a shaping vision in spite of public hostility and neglect. "Crab-Angel" recalls the satire in "Lunar Baedeker" and "Lions' Jaws" of the posing and lavish costume of the pseudo-artist, here imaged as a dwarf who rides atop a "monster-stallion" in Ringling's "revolving / trinity   of circus attractions." In his own fantasies the dwarf may possess power and talent, but he is only an "Automaton bare-back rider" whose soaring flights into circus skies are on wires manipulated by the circus master. The poem is a series of colorful images that convey the fantasy world of the dwarf as well as his helplessness and sexual ambiguity. More than in any other of Mina Loy's poems brilliance of image dominates the satire: the dwarf seems "Something the contour / of a captured crab / waving its useless pearly claws"; "An iridescent speck / dripped from a rainbow / onto an ebony cloud"; "Helen of Lilliput? / Hercules in a powder puff?" These glittering comic conjectures give way in the final stanza to the dwarf's reality. His flight stops and he

> subsides like an ironic sigh
> to the soft earth
> and ploughs
> his bow-legged way
> laboriously   towards the exit
> waving a yellow farewell with his perruque

Representing ironic defensiveness, lack of vitality, and artificiality, the dwarf is an ironic diminution of the alienated artist depicted in Théodore Banville's "Le Saut du Tremplin" (1857). This poem "relates the mental triumph of the poet-clown who seeks to emancipate himself from the crass contingencies of an ugly and limited existence":

> Enfin de son vil échafaud,
> Le clown sauta si haut, si haut,

> Qu'il creva le plafond de toiles
> Au son du cor et du tambour,
> Et, le coeur dévoré d'amour,
> Alla rouler dans les étoiles.[12]

Clearly playing upon Banville's theme and imagery, "Crab-Angel" transforms a cliché of literary history into a fresh, visual delight.

As regards the subject matter of her poetry, Mina Loy rejects, except for satire, the sensuality and grotesquerie of the Decadents and the preference of art for art's sake and Parnassian poets for subjects of acknowledged beauty. The latter filled their poems with evocations of ancient and exotic cultures, art objects, and the fierce grace of animals. While Mina Loy does write a few poems on works of art, her subjects are usually the strivings and disappointments of average or destitute humanity. She does not believe that the ugly is beautiful but that the artist's vision can infuse the ugly or commonplace with beauty. She would, like Baudelaire, given mud, transform it into gold ("Tu m'as donne ta boue et j'en ai fait de l'or").[13] Her objective is dramatized in *Anglo-Mongrels*, where three children embody contrasting attitudes toward art. Esau, child prodigy and "'Infant Aesthete,'" poses in Decadent draperies in his family's drawing room before admiring adults assembled in his honor:

> The boy   one bare arm
> Thrust through a gossamer
> toga   of Tyrian rose
> is holding out an orb

The drawing room itself is an eclectic tribute to antique beauty:

12. "Finally, from the cheap scaffolding, / The clown jumped so high, so high, / That he broke the starry ceiling / To the sound of the horn and the drum, / And, the heart devoured by love, / Went rolling among the stars." Denommé, *The French Parnassian Poets*, 74.

13. Quoted in Starkie, *From Gautier to Eliot*, 34.

> The fire   flicks from the
> fifteenth-century
> andirons   and the ruby eyes
> of Buddha
> On treasures of Thibet
> the 'trousered' draperies
> of a wood faced Virgin from the Netherlands
>
> The golden wings
> of Florentine angels
> and a piece of Ming

Ova, the poem's middle-class heroine and Loy's surrogate, derives her aesthetic stimulation from the beauty hidden in life's refuse and necessity. She must

> coerce the shy
> Spirit of Beauty
> from excrements and physic—
>
> While Esau of Ridover Square
> absorbs the erudite idea
> that Beauty is nowhere
> except posthumously to itself
> in the antique

Against Esau's worship of the exquisite beauty of antiquity and Ova's hesitant gropings in the muck of actuality, Colossus defies all artistic and social traditions. A caricature of Arthur Cravan, Mina Loy's second husband (as Esau seems to caricature her first), Colossus battles to destroy all proscriptions:

> the first time
> he opens his eyes
> wittingly—
> 'Tis like an eagle
> soaring on the sun
> and the first time
> he communes within himself

> he decides
> All words are lies

The revolt of Colossus against social convention is itself an artistic gesture. His mother having brought him into the drawing
room to show him off, he throws

> the tea—pot
> at Mme Follilot
> because her top-knot
> displeases him so

> AND who
> would care to call at
> any house   on finding the young master in the hall
> pissing into our reverend pastor's hat?

Colossus represents the art-for-art's-sake defiance of convention carried to the destructive extreme of Dada. Loy sympa-
thizes with the Dada trend in twentieth-century art, especially
its encouragement of artistic experiment; but Dada's nihilistic
current runs counter to her essentially constructive quest. She
strives for beautiful form created by close attention to style and
based on the modernist paradox, discussed in Chapter Three, of
simultaneous destruction and creation.

Of Mina Loy's borrowings from art for art's sake, her applica-
tion of its defense of artistic autonomy to modernist abstraction
(and experiment in general) is especially important. From the
art-for-art's-sake emphasis on form and style, its divorce of nature and art, and its contempt for the public's preferences, it is a
short step to appreciation of an esoteric, abstract art that in sub-
suming subject matter under the formal properties of a work
leaves the public baffled and angry. Loy gives her most thor-
ough explanation and justification of nonrealistic art in the *Lunar Baedeker* poems on individual artists. The poem "Poe" may at
first seem out of place among tributes to Constantin Brancusi,
James Joyce, and Wyndham Lewis, but the inclusion of Poe is

justified by the fact that his defense of beauty, like that of his admirer Baudelaire, lays the groundwork for the abandonment of literal realism. Baudelaire argued (*e.g.*, his *Salon de 1859*) that art is not an imitation of nature but the imagination applied to nature to create a higher nonnatural spiritual beauty. Similarly, Poe in "The Philosophy of Composition" (1846) makes beauty "the sole legitimate province of the poem." In "Poe" Mina Loy evokes such an artificial beauty. As noted in Chapter Three, a chill, elegant diction cleansed of the didacticism and sentimentality usually associated with death parallels Poe's treatment of death, death being the subject he advocated as most conducive to sadness, sadness the tone most effective in attaining beauty.

Thus, in "Poe" and "Apology of Genius" Loy, like other explicators of modernism, establishes the preeminence of beauty and the superiority of the artificial or nonnatural.[14] In elaborating her aesthetic she instructs the audience on "how to read" abstract art. In the unpublished essay "The Metaphysical Pattern in Aesthetics" she proposes that modern art be approached as a map of the artist's personality without the obfuscation of a subject. In her Gertrude Stein article she notes the responsibility of the observer to creatively encounter the work of art. Art provides the stimulus which, "although it proceeds from a complete aesthetic organisation, leaves us unlimited latitude for personal response." Modern art has abandoned external appearances to seek the "nucleus of being," and has found abstract forms the most honest and provocative conveyors of the artist's vision:

14. See Georges Braque, in "The Wild Men of Paris," an interview conducted by Gelett Burgess in *Architectural Record*, New York (May, 1910), 405, in Edward F. Fry (ed.), *Cubism* (New York: McGraw-Hill, n.d.), 53. Braque explains his abstract paintings in terms similar to Loy's: "I couldn't portray a woman in all her natural loveliness . . . I haven't the skill. No one has. I must, therefore, create a new sort of beauty, the beauty that appears to me in terms of volume, of line, of mass, of weight, and through that beauty interpret my subjective impression. Nature is a mere pretext for a decorative composition, plus sentiment. It suggests emotion, and I translate that emotion into art. I want to expose the Absolute, and not merely the factitious woman."

Perhaps the ideal enigma that the modern would desire to solve, is, what would we know about anything, if we didn't know anything about it . . . To track intellection back to the embryo.

For the spiritual record of the race is this nostalgia for the crystallization of the irreducible surplus of the abstract. The bankruptcy of mysticism declared itself in an inability to locate this divine irritation, and the burden of its debt to the evolution of consciousness has devolved on abstract art.

The search for the "divine irritation" involves a democratization of subject matter, the use of the commonplace. Modern art, Mina Loy continues in a development of the view of art represented by Ova, extends aesthetic sensibility into the "flux of life . . . pouring its aesthetic aspect into your eyes, your ears—and you ignore it because you are looking for your canons of beauty in some sort of frame or glass case of tradition." Cubism discovered the aesthetic qualities of the newspaper, Cézanne of the plate, Brancusi of the egg, and Gertrude Stein of the "Word." [15]

The tributes to contemporary nonrealists in *Lunar Baedeker* are very Parnassian in their idealization of the art object as the embodiment of beauty; but unlike Leconte de Lisle, leader of the Parnassians who turned to the cold, dead splendor of ancient art for his "Venus de Milo," Mina Loy evokes the essence of art by living artists who in their turn have probed nature for the "divine irritation" and then given form to their vision. Joyce presents "The word made flesh / and feeding upon itself / with erudite fangs"; in abstract sculpture Brancusi penetrates nature to reveal "the nucleus of flight"; and Lewis has transformed the "human mist" into cubistic abstractions of eternity, "pyramidical survivors / in the cyclorama of space." Of these tributes "Brancusi's Golden Bird" most clearly reflects Loy's debt to Parnassian attitudes and develops her defense of abstract art. The brass sculpture, cousin of Yeats's golden bird, glistens from the poem in an eloquent proclamation of art's divine achievement.

15. Loy, "Gertrude Stein," 429–30.

Brancusi has freshly intuited "the nucleus of flight" and then imbued his vision in a lump of metal.

The poem was printed in the *Dial* juxtaposed to a photograph of the *Golden Bird* and was intended as a comment on the sculpture. Gilbert Seldes, managing editor of the *Dial*, wrote to Scofield Thayer, the editor, that the only controversy arose over the poem.[16] Although Seldes does not explain the hostile response, the court dispute (1926–1928) as to whether the sculpture should be allowed entry into the United States as a work of art suggests an answer. Brancusi declared the *Golden Bird* a work of art worth $600; New York Customs said it was merely a piece of metal and slapped a $210 duty on it. Witnesses for Customs argued that the work was abstract and gave no aesthetic pleasure and therefore that it did not merit the status of art.[17] In her poem Mina Loy disdainfully anticipates this blind conventionalism by deifying the abstract work of art and its creator. Backers of Brancusi understood her praise and included the poem in the catalog of his first major American exhibit, held in New York at the Brummer Gallery in 1926 (Alfred Stieglitz, in 1914, had given Brancusi a one-man show at "291").

The poem opens with an equation of the art object to a toy, of the artist to God:

> The toy
> become the aesthetic archetype
>
> As if
> some patient peasant God
> had rubbed and rubbed
> the Alpha and Omega
> of Form
> into a lump of metal

16. Nicholas Joost, *Scofield Thayer and the Dial: An Illustrated History* (Carbondale: Southern Illinois University Press, 1964), 110.

17. Carola Giedion-Welcker, *Constantin Brancusi*, trans. Maria Jolas and Anne Leroy (New York: George Braziller, 1959), 212–17.

The first image suggests the spirit of play that inspired many modern artists as well as the deceptive childlike simplicity of much of their art. This simplicity, Brancusi said, "is complexity itself, and one has to be nourished by its essence in order to understand its value." [18] The child, the primitive, the abstract artist—each in his effort to discover life's essence strips away superfluity; the brass bird may be toy, goddess (Mina Loy says it is as "bare as the brow of Osiris"), art. The analogy of artist and peasant God draws upon the nineteenth-century equation of God's creation of man from a lump of clay to the artist's abstraction of form from nature. The peasant God, also a reference to Brancusi's peasant origins in Rumania, images the effort of primitive man and artist to extract meaning from amorphousness. Alpha and Omega are the elusive answers to the mysteries of existence momentarily and everlastingly arrested in form by the artist-God. The plosives of "patient peasant" and their *b* cognate in the repeated "rubbed" enact the craftsman's careful exertion, the patience and tenacity, necessary to the creative act. "As if," extended beyond the rest of the poem to emphasize the hypothetical nature of the artist-God analogy, indicates that Loy knew H. Vaihinger's *The Philosophy of 'As If'* (1913). Vaihinger's theory that art is a transitory fiction imposed upon reality resembles Loy's belief that the art object is the brief intuition of form within chaos. With "as if" she acknowledges that her analogy is, like Brancusi's brass metaphor for flight, only what seems at one moment the most truthful account of the artistic act. [19]

The poem's defense and explanation of abstract art contain passages that verge upon pure sound: the sculpture is "an incandescent curve / licked by chromatic flames / in labyrinths of

---

18. *Ibid.*, 220.
19. Frank Kermode, *The Sense of an Ending: Studies in the Theory of Fiction* (New York: Oxford University Press, 1967), 39–41, discusses Vaihinger's theory.

reflections." Here Loy achieves what she admires in Brancusi. As he modeled the essence of flight in brass, she evokes the essence of his sculpture in passages of sound. Brancusi's metal shape does not delineate the visual specifics of flight; her poem is not a literal description of the sculpture. Both are involved in synesthesia: the poem's patterns of sound stimulate our visual and tactile senses to the heat, light, color, and texture of the golden bird.

The final stanza returns to the divinity of art and the beauty of abstract simplicity:

> The immaculate
> conception
> of the inaudible bird
> occurs
> in gorgeous reticence———

The pun "immaculate / conception" implies both the divinity of the art object and the purity of its origin in the mind of the sculptor. For all that it "shrills," the "inaudible bird" does not sing a natural song; it is not an imitation of nature. Like nature it simply "occurs." "Gorgeous reticence" completes the evocation of the sculpture. Alone "gorgeous" is trite and florid, "reticence" is brittle and fussy; combined they emanate refined splendor.

Brancusi, Joyce, Lewis, and Poe are exemplars of the artistic ideal and, more important, of human fulfillment. They have exercised vision with integrity. Mina Loy returns to the theme of artistic vision in "Jules Pascin" and "Stravinski's Flute" (1958), both slighter poems than the evocations of artistic excellence in *Lunar Baedeker*. "Pascin" eulogizes the man; "Stravinski's Flute," like the earlier poems, evokes the man's artistry:

> The swan's neck stiffens
> and the swan

> starts from the swamps of Silence
>
> A voice-evangel of loud ice
> soars through a cloven dome

Stravinski's accomplishment is to transcend the pain and chaos of time and carry the listener to paradise, called Elysium and Nirvana:

> Elysian whistler
> trailing a strand of sound
> to fluted altitude
>
> as from a Hindu's hand is flung
> a rope into Nirvana.

This late poem continues a major theme that originates in "Parturition," whose speaker desires to transcend biological process and merge with cosmic becoming (Bergsonian *durée*). As we remember, her momentary transcendence brings a disturbing vision of personal insignificance, and eventually the I who speaks for Mina Loy resigns herself to existence within the flux of time. However, the return to the theme of transcendence in the poems on art suggests that the desire for transcendence was a significant component of Loy's psychology, metaphysics, and aesthetics. If, as Edith Cobb says, artists "return in memory [to childhood] in order to renew the power and impulse to create at its very source," then the autobiographical child Ova may enact Mina Loy's initial consciousness of ecstasy in the escape from time and locate the origin of her time-space orientation.[20] Having been unjustly humiliated by her parents, Ova flees to the garden where she has an "illumination":

> The high—skies
> have come gently upon her
> and all their
> steadfast light is shining out of her

---

20. Edith Cobb,"The Ecology of Imagination in Childhood," *Daedalus*, LXXX-VIII, (1959), 539, 545.

> She is conscious
> not through her body   but through space

Because Ova is human her bliss is short-lived: a chicken egg breaks on the garden path, "a horrible / aborted contour / a yellow murder / in a viscous pool." Although Ova cannot yet interpret the symbolism of the broken egg, she feels a "contraction" to the "uneasiness" of this world's biological process and disillusion. Mina Loy, the mature Ova, realizing the difficulty of attaining and the impossibility of sustaining transcendence, makes her personal need an element of the human condition. In her later poetry she turns from the artists who can momentarily transcend time to the bum. Imbued with the seemingly innate human urge for transcendence, for beauty and meaning, the bum lacks the discipline to sustain honest vision and so pursues false Nirvanas.

II   *The Bum*   Love the hideous in order to find the
sublime core of it.
—"Aphorisms on Futurism"

The common tragedy is to have suffered
without having 'appeared.'
—Untitled poem (1962)

The group of poems that focus on the bum and the other denizens of the city's hostile streets forms Mina Loy's version of the *Tableaux parisiens* of Baudelaire. (One remembers that her early paintings were compared to those of Constantin Guys, whose depictions of city life inspired the *Tableaux*.) Her subjects are the city's human refuse, individuals who have exchanged disciplined vision for the easier gratifications of alcohol and sloth, or who have been blinded by the abasements of poverty. Loy strives to embrace and illuminate these individuals through the sunrays of her poet's vision. The identification of sun and poet, drawn from Baudelaire's "Le Soleil,"[21] is implicit in "Perlun"

21.   Quand, ainsi qu'un poète, il descend dans les villes,
Il ennoblit le sort des choses les plus viles,

(1921), a personification of the sun as a raffish, juvenile deity "Holding in immaculate arms / the syphilitic sailor / on his avoided death bunk / or the movie vamp / among the muffled shadows of the shrubberies—— / / Picking lemons in Los Angeles   broke." As Perlun, Loy raises forgotten specimens of failed human aspiration to visibility and significance, thereby completing her metaphysics. She also implements the aesthetic principle set forth in *Anglo-Mongrels* that the artist must seek beauty in life's commonplaces and its excrement.

The prominent urban setting in these poems accents a minor motif of the earlier poetry. Loy's reliance on the urban landscape must rest in the fact of her own largely urban existence. She lived in London, Munich, Paris, Florence, and New York; and her travels took her to Geneva, Mexico City, Buenos Aires, Rio de Janeiro, and Vienna. For her, nature seems merely a poetic convention to which one retires for recuperation. Her literary heritage—Baudelaire, Gautier, Laforgue, Apollinaire, Marinetti —employs the urban landscape; and like other American moderns who drew upon these authors, Mina Loy seems to find the city as subject a means of revolt against the romantic preoccupation with nature.[22] For a poet of 1914 who insisted, as Mina Loy did, on an honest poetry of the present, the city's civilized beauty and horror, its social complexity and visual excitement, demanded attention. Furthermore, the city's perpetual activity provided a context and metaphor for human becoming. "To You" (1916), intended as the introduction to the *Love Songs*, images this aspect: "The city / Wedged between impulse and unfolding / Bridged / By diurnal splintering / Of egos." In the meta-

---

Et s'introduit en roi, sans bruit et sans valets,

Dans tous les hôpitaux et dans tous les palais.

Baudelaire, "Le Soleil," *Les Fleurs du Mal*, 92. "When, just like a poet, he descends to the cities, / He ennobles the fate of the vilest things, / And he enters like a king, without noise and without valets, / All the hospitals and all the palaces."

22. Perkins, *A History of Modern Poetry*, 300–304.

physical quest the city also provides environmental obstacles to selfhood. The city is a hell where "Lit cavities in the face of the city / Open their glassy embrace to receive you"; and in "Hot Cross Bum" the Bowery dances with hellish flames:

> Beyond a hell-vermilion
> curtain of neon
> lies the Bowery
>
> a lurid lane
> leading misfortune's monsters
>
> the human . . . race
> altered to irrhythmic stagger
>
> along the alcoholic's
> exit to Ecstasia.

In the early poetry the city unobtrusively offers a variety of personalities and experiences. The sequence "Three Moments in Paris" (1915) —"Café du Néant," "Magasins du Louvre," and "One O'Clock at Night"—depicts youthful nihilists, Parisian cocottes and shop girls, and intellectuals, all of whom have gravitated to the city's freedom and stimulation. The girls and matrons of the poems of female selfhood lead urban lives, if only because their functions are restricted to houses bound by streets surging with masculine energy. The poems "To You," "Sketch of a Man on a Platform," and "Lions' Jaws" satirize urbanized and Futurist male activity. "The Black Virginity" and "The Dead" draw upon the city for their settings and images; "The Costa San Giorgio" is a tribute to urban dynamism.

In the post–1920 poems the urban environment becomes even more prominent, although the emphasis is on the lives shaped by the city. The city as microcosm of cosmic and social forces is most explicit in the *Lunar Baedeker* poem "Der Blinde Junge" where a physically blinded youth is emblematic of the frustrated human need for vision. The poem is descended from Baudelaire's "Les Aveugles" and especially Théophile Gautier's "L'Aveugle." The blind youth of Mina Loy's poem, like his predecessors, is trapped in the eternal darkness that means spiritual damnation. Like "l'aveugle" of Gautier who strives for self-expression on a flute, the blind youth plays a mouth-organ. However, the mouth-organ speaks only his incompleteness and the folly of the "illuminati" who have sight but cannot see. The youth's blindness, symbolic of humanity in general and perhaps the postwar generation in particular, prophesies the spiritual atrophy that afflicts the self when vision is abandoned or obstructed. He is society's— the city's—victim; but the larger arena of his tragedy is an indifferent universe, represented in all Mina Loy's poetry by the sun. To fulfill his being, man must look unflinchingly into the sun, but one of the realities he will perceive is that it cares nothing for him:

> The dam Bellona
> littered
> her eyeless offspring
> Kriegsopfer
> upon the pavements of Vienna
>
> Sparkling precipitate
> the spectral day
> involves
> the visionless obstacle
>
> this slow blind face
> pushing
> its virginal nonentity
> against the light
>
> Pure purposeless eremite
> of centripetal sentience
>
> Upon the carnose horologe of the ego
> the vibrant tendon index moves not
>
> Since the black lightning desecrated
> the retinal altar
>
> Void and extinct
> this planet of the soul

strains from the craving throat
in static flight upslanting

A downy youth's snout
nozzling the sun
drowned in dumbfounded instinct

Listen!
illuminati of the coloured earth
How this expressionless "thing"
blows out damnation and concussive dark

Upon a mouth-organ

According to the cosmological imagery of the poem, the self
ought to be a planet circling the parent sun, but without sight
the self is doomed to extinction: it degenerates to an animal or a
thing. With these images and that of the retinal altar, "Der
Blinde Junge" becomes the key diagram of Mina Loy's metaphysics and firmly unites her to the Baudelairian–*fin de siècle*
emphasis on vision. The preoccupation is captured in the litho-
graph by French Symbolist painter Odilon Redon, *L'Oeil comme
un Balloon bizarre se dirige vers L'Infini* (1882). In the painting a
huge eyeball traverses the cosmos like a helium balloon from
which the upper half of a human head is suspended. All the
cognitive powers of the head are subsumed by the giant exploratory and, for Mina Loy, intuitive eye.

If the blind youth represents humanity betrayed by society's
irresponsibility, the bum—the most prominent figure in Loy's
tableaus of the metropolis—represents self-willed delusion.
Lacking the discipline to pursue selfhood, he hides from reality
in chimeras that parallel the cocaine and costume of the insincere artist. Loy compares the bum, as she has the failed artist, to
a clown. In the *Love Songs* the speaker laments that within an
indifferent cosmos individuals become clownish by virtue of
their inadequate, archaic humanity: they are "Foetal buffoons /
. . . . / Stringing emotions / Looped aloft." The bum carries this

hapless inadequacy to the extreme. In "Ignoramus" (*ca.* 1915/
1923), a poem placed with "Crab-Angel" and "Der Blinde Junge"
in *Lunar Baedeker*, he is a "Clown of Fortune" reminiscent of
Chaplin's Little Tramp and precursor of Hart Crane's "Chaplin-
esque." Unable to compete in the counting houses of men, he has
taken a seat in nature's stock exchange, where he trades in in-
substantial "glumes" and avoids his own failure by fastidiously
mimicking the postures and speech of the world's "busymen."
His destiny is to possess a sense of martyrdom and an avidity in-
commensurate with his ability to act:

> breakfasting on rain
> You hurry
> To interpolate
> The over-growth
> Of vegetation
> With a walking stick
>
> Or smear a friend
> With a greasy residuum
> From boiling your soul down
> You can walk to Empyrean to-gether
> Under the same
> Oil-silk umbrella

Of the other two poems depicting the bum, "Lady Laura in
Bohemia" (1924/1931) is a colorful portrait of one of the lost generation. Laura is a socialite "Trained in a circus of swans" who
has made "somersault descent / into the half-baked under-
world." In this lowly ring of the human circus she, like Ignoramus, parodies the rituals of the respectable world. She is an
"abbess-prostitute" who "presides / Jazz-Mass / / the gin-fizz eucharist dispenses":

> Her hell is
> Zelli's
>
> Where she floods the bar
> with all her curls

> in the delirious tears from those bill-poster eyes
> plastering 'court proceedings' on the wall
> of her inconsiderable soul

"Hot Cross Bum" analyzes at length the Bowery derelicts who so captured Mina Loy's imagination that she made them her neighbors. They are "misfortune's monsters" seeking through fraudulent means the blissful transcendence of life. Instead of vision, they employ alcohol as their means to "Ecstasia," "Elysium," "Nirvana":

> Hoary rovers
> ignoring all but despicable directions
> shift through intentional trend of busymen
>
> Their sailing, flailing limbs
> of disequilibrium
>
> clutching at wobbly banisters
> to Elysium

The bum desires the same divine flight that led Brancusi to create "the nucleus of flight," Joyce an "Empyrean emporium," and Lewis "geometric Chimeras." But, lacking self-discipline, he relies on delusory "crystal horizons" shaped by "a Brilliance all of bottles."

Between the extremes of artist and bum exists most of humanity, striving for the necessary saving illusion and seeking beauty, like Ova, within life's nondescript or jaded offerings. Mina Loy is especially attracted by the efforts of the poor, more the victims of society than a lack of self-discipline. The poor of "On Third Avenue: Part 2" (1958) find beauty in the tawdry glitter of a tower-shaped box office "before a ten-cent Cinema": "Like an electric fungus / sprung from its own effulgence / of intercircled jewelry / reflected on the pavement." They momentarily forget their bleak lives in "the brilliancy / of a trolley / loaded with luminous busts." Another type of transcendence is represented by the Jewish showman of "Hilarious Israel" who transforms racial victimization into Broadway glitter. Escaped from massacre and inhospitable foster cultures, "Magnet to maniac / misfortune," he rises a "Phoenix of Exodus," "messiah / of our amusement":

> What esoteric "tic"
> transforms
> metallic thorns of succorless fosterlands
> to pastel limbs of chorus-girls in bloom;
>
> the blood on pogrom exits
> to rubies of pomegranates
> on costume?

The transplantation from Wailing Wall to Broadway requires sedation of vision: "Coma of logic / myopia of ire." The Jew has had to accept "spurious horizons," but he has escaped the bum's debasement. As phoenix and messiah he has created— like the artist—a saving illusion, but still he is a somewhat ironic figure, not quite all that his people had hoped for.

The old woman of "Chiffon Velours" (1947) is nearly beyond any of mankind's evasions, and indeed it is the observer, not the old woman, who has a momentary transforming vision. A companion to Baudelaire's "Vieilles,"

> She is sere.
>
> Her features,
> verging on a shriek
> reviling age,
>
> flee from death in odd directions
> somehow retained by a web of wrinkles.

She is a model of the "last creation" and also the "original design / of destitution." Poverty deprives her of any worldly defense against time, making her the unretouched picture of our common death. But an illusion briefly gilds the old woman's stark reality as her skirt, reflecting the filth of the gutter, becomes an elegant fabric:

> Trimmed with one sudden burst
> of flowery cotton
> half her black skirt
> glows as a soiled mirror;
> reflects the gutter—
> a yard of chiffon velours.

The poem returns to the conclusions of "The Black Virginity." The only affirmation of the absolute available to the I-eye is fleeting images (intuitions) of beauty. Yet these images are often ambiguous. Just as in the *Love Songs* images of romantic love slyly shift to pornographic grimaces, so in "Chiffon Velours" beauty and the filth of the gutter are entangled. The beauty that flits across this omen of death is ironically the reflection of a degraded universe. Has the eye intuited cosmic good or evil? Only the artist's ability to give that intuition form argues for the positive interpretation.

The child's fantasy world in "Ephemerid" dramatizes the necessary reliance on illusions and illustrates that beauty may be gleaned from closely attending to life's shifting images: "The Eternal is sustained by serial metamorphosis, / even so Beauty is." The speaker witnesses such a metamorphosis as a gigantic insect becomes a little girl dressed in an old curtain. "Penury / with dream," the child exemplifies the meagerness of mankind's means for realizing its dreams, as well as the beauty that often emanates from its effort. Mina Loy, characteristically, does not detail the substance of her intuition of the eternal, only the fact that the visionary act itself is of value. The fantasizing child lifts "the eyelids; / to whisper of subvisual resources / in the uncolor of the unknown."

The beauty of the child, the old woman, the Jewish showman, or even of the defeated bum goes largely unremarked. They "have suffered / without having 'appeared.'" The poem supplying these lines adds that a martyr's anguish is mitigated by the public's admiration. But no attention is paid unexceptional individuals. The pathos of their situation is increased, as *Anglo-Mongrels* explains in regard to Ova's growing self-consciousness, by the "inattentive audience / of the Infinite." No kindly, or even hostile, eye returns the human stare into the universe, and neglected by man and the infinite, the self's clownishness increases. Fulfilling the role she has set for the artist, Mina Loy aims in her later poetry to bestow significance on suffering and failure, to raise mankind above its clownishness by finding beauty in the cosmic struggle.

Epilogue

This study has sought to introduce the poetry of Mina Loy and to suggest its merit. In drawing these purposes to conclusion I would like to consider directly the question: Why, then, is Mina Loy an *American* poet? To summarize the preceding chapters, three links to the American modernists seem essential to any answer. First, in her awareness that the subjects and structures of English poetry in 1910 were inadequate to experience, Mina Loy anticipates the Americans in drawing upon French literature of the art-for-art's-sake tradition for the justification and practice of her poetic revolt. As justification it taught the supremacy of art and contempt for the bourgeois fear of the new. But as her satires of the tradition and her praise of artistic responsibility indicate, she condemns the pose of artistic alienation. Implicit in her poetry is the notion of the poet as seer—the poet of Emerson and Whitman—who guides the way to divine self-realization. Certainly her emphasis on the self harkens back to American romanticism although its origins are not necessarily American. In terms of the practice of literature, the French tradition emphasized the craft of poetry and encouraged experiment. It also offered a greater freedom of subject: the seamy and mundane aspects of life as well as the sexual fantasies and subconscious terrors of the self became available to the poet. Within this tradition Jules Laforgue provides Mina Loy—as he does Ezra Pound, T. S. Eliot, and Wallace Stevens—a cure for clichéd sentimentalism. The sophisticated irony of Laforgue's Pierrot serves as a model for disdaining social ritual and expressing emotion.[1]

1. René Taupin, *L'Influence du Symbolisme Français sur la Poésie Américaine, de 1910 à 1920* (Paris: Librairie Ancienne Honoré Champion, 1929), 152–55, 225–32,

Laforgue of course introduces the second and perhaps the most important link between Mina Loy and the Americans: a verbalism that in some of its manifestations Pound calls logopoeia. Like the Americans she employs a compressed diction that abandons the poetic commonplace and demands the total involvement of the reader in the poem's language; indifferent to poetic eloquence, this diction reflects modes of perception and utilizes the spoken language. More at home with abstractions than some of the Americans, Mina Loy nevertheless shares their creation of (sometimes arbitrary) word-worlds that do not depend on previous explanations of experience. Among the Americans Marianne Moore employs a "crystalline structure" that conveys the integrity of her vision and of the "perceived world's multifarious otherness" in careful symmetries of language. William Carlos Williams depicts the world's processes and independent thingness—"no ideas but in things"—in words cleansed of the corrosion of habit, while Wallace Stevens, the philosopher, constructs whimsical fictions—the world's only order—from word games.[2] Even more radical, Gertrude Stein in *Tender Buttons* liberates words from denotation to form nearly abstract word patterns. As her contribution to these experiments Loy causes words to express the movement of consciousness over and into the human quest for significance. As with the Americans her verbalism, at its best, shapes vividly fresh images and exact descriptions, finding its rhythms in the movement of the mind's eye rather than in conventional metric. In short, her poetry illustrates American modernism as René Taupin early defined it. This poetry, he says, observes even among non-Imagist poets the tenants of Imagism—conciseness and exactness, use of the image, composition by musical phrase: "Tous ces poètes, qu'ils soient

discusses the influence of Laforgue on Pound and Eliot and, by implication, on American modernism in general.

2. Hugh Kenner, *A Homemade World: The American Modernist Writers* (New York: Knopf, 1975), discusses the arbitrary word structure of the Americans; the references to Marianne Moore are on pp. 102 and 114.

ou plus imagistes, ou plus verbalistes ou plus musicaux, possè-
dent ces trois qualités."[3] Taupin views these qualities as French
in origin, and when Pound attributes to Mina Loy (and Marianne Moore) the "arid clarity . . . of le tempérament de l'Americaine" he points to the French lesson of honest and unsentimen-
tal diction.

Finally, Mina Loy is linked to the Americans by her translation
into poetry of the techniques and structures of modern European painting, especially Futurism and Cubism. Gertrude Stein,
at times a verbal Cubist, is famous for her patronage of modern
art; and Marianne Moore, Stevens, and Williams were interested in painting. This interest, fed by contact in New York City
with the new art, influenced their experiments with image and
structure. Loy's distinction is that, as much a painter as a poet,
she appears in the American little magazines of 1914 with the
innovations of the painters already assimilated into her poetry.
Historically she is among the first English-language poets to
adopt the techniques of modern painting, especially fragmentation and collage juxtaposition, and to tie these to the age's "crisis
in consciousness."[4] Poetry had to make sense of a radically
changing world and to depict new modes of perception. Hesitation would have meant a personal and artistic failure of vision.

Mina Loy's tragedy as a poet is that although she was among
the first to respond innovatively to the crises of the new century,
she lacked the discipline, or desire, to carry her innovations
much beyond their culmination in *Lunar Baedeker* and *Anglo-
Mongrels and the Rose*. Later poems portend a major development of her theme, but they do not break through to new structures for conveying the I-eye's relation to existence; in fact, they

3. "All these poets, whether imagists, verbalists or poets for whom poetry is
music, possess these three qualities." Taupin, *L'Influence du Symbolisme Française*,
278.
4. David Antin, "Modernism and Postmodernism: Approaching the Present
in American Poetry," *Boundary 2*, I (1972), 106–109, 120–21, and *passim*, characterizes collage as a definitive trait of modernist poetry that is picked up by the
postmodernists.

abandon some of the most daring of her early experiments. This failure may be due to her sense that poetry was but a hand-maiden to the business of living. The attitude prompts the question she put to her publisher Jonathan Williams: "'But, why do you waste your time on these thoughts of mine—I was never a poet?'"[5] The reader is unlikely to share her self-disparagement. Mina Loy may have lacked a sense of vocation but for over a decade, fired by self-awakening and the excitement of the age's artistic revolt, her poetic genius met the criterion she set for the artist of giving meaningful form to chaos.

Speculation on what direction Mina Loy might have taken had she been dedicated to poetry helps to place her in the currents of American poetry as they spill into the present. While her early poetry contains overtones of Prufrockian despair, she does not move with Eliot and his descendants among the poets and critics of the New Criticism into religious, political, and artistic conservatism. Rather, her theme of vision and her disavowal of absolutes, her depictions of consciousness, and her tolerance of experiment situate her, as I have suggested, with Stein, Pound, and Williams as a precursor of postmodernism or, more specifically, of poets such as Kenneth Rexroth, the Beats, and Charles Olson and the Black Mountain poets. (These poets, according to Rexroth, continue the French tradition, minus the symbolists and Laforgue.)[6] The connection Mina Loy forges in her imagery between (female) sexuality and the unconscious looks to surrealist, confessional, and feminist poetry. Her use of collage, fragmentation, and free verse anticipates the composition by field proposed in Olson's "Projective Verse." "The Costa San Giorgio," drawing upon Futurist dynamism, parallels the Projectivist depiction of a world in flux with the I become a part

5. Jonathan Williams, promotion letter for the Jargon Society, Aspen, Colorado, July 5, 1969, p. 2.
6. Kenneth Rexroth, "Disengagement: The Art of the Beat Generation," in *A Casebook on the Beat*, ed. Thomas Parkinson (New York: Thomas Y. Crowell, 1961), 190–91.

of the world's thingness. However, unlike many of the poets in Olson's orbit, Mina Loy gives up her attempt to place the I within the flux; she does not wish to diminish the ego, or self, but through the intuitions and cerebrations of the self to arrive at tentative explanations of existence. She strives not for "escape from the self" but for self-realization.[7] Furthermore, the theme of the escape from time which runs throughout her poetry reflects a desire for transcendence of this world, not for oneness with it. The desire triumphs in her poems on art. Here she joins those modernists who step out of time into the fixed, spatialized realm of the work of art. But she relinquishes this dream of nirvana, for in her later poetry on common humanity she acknowledges the near impossibility of such transcendence and shares the existentialist commitment to responsible human action in the time of this world, action embodied for her in vision.[8] On the basis of her movement in this direction an existentialist-feminist poetry employing organic forms seems best to fulfill the emphases of her poetry.

But speculation on how Mina Loy might have developed her themes and structures needs to be limited to clarifying and appreciating the achievement of the poetry she actually wrote. What emerges is a poetry that earns our recognition partially by its original and honest response to modernity. More important, her poetry demonstrates the fine attunement to the possibilities

7. The phrase is the title of Karl Malkoff's *Escape from the Self: A Study in Contemporary Poetry and Poetics* (New York: Columbia University Press, 1977), a discussion of confessional and projectivist poetry. The diminution of the self in postmodern literature is also considered by Charles Altieri, "From Symbolist Thought to Immanence: The Ground of Postmodern American Poetics," *Boundary 2*, I (1973), *passim*.

8. The distinction between modernist spatialization, projectivism, and existentialism is made by William V. Spanos in "Modern Literary Criticism and the Spatialization of Time: An Existential Critique," *Journal of Aesthetics and Art Criticism*, XXIX (1970), 87–104; "The Detective and the Boundary: Some Notes on the Postmodern Literary Imagination," *Boundary 2*, I (1972), 147–68; and "Heidegger, Kierkegaard, and the Hermeneutic Circle: Towards a Postmodern Theory of Interpretation as Dis-closure," *Boundary 2*, IV (1976), 445–88.

for words that raises the poet above other practitioners of language. By this quality Mina Loy merits inclusion among the distinguished poets of the twentieth century.

Published Writings of Mina Loy

This bibliography contains all of Mina Loy's published writing that I have been able to locate. Not included are the many unpublished poems, plays, and prose works in the Collection of American Literature at the Beinecke Rare Book and Manuscript Library, Yale University. Some unpublished writing also remains in the possession of Loy's daughters. For each work I give the first place and date of publication, and I indicate if it has appeared in one of the volumes of Loy's poems—*Lunar Baedeker* (Dijon: Contact Publishing Co., 1923) and *Lunar Baedeker & Time-Tables* (Highlands, N.C.: Jonathan Williams, 1958). These volumes are now collectors' items, and most of the little magazines and anthologies that published individual poems can be found only in major research libraries. Thus, readers interested in going beyond the sampling of poems I have provided in this study can look forward to another collection of Loy's poems being prepared by Jonathan Williams, publisher of *Lunar Baedeker & Time-Tables*.

POETRY

"Aid of the Madonna." *Accent*, VII (1947), 111.

Anglo-Mongrels and the Rose. First half, *Little Review*, IX (Spring, 1923), 10–18; IX (Autumn–winter, 1923–24), 41–51; second half, *Contact Collection of Contemporary Writers*. Paris: Three Mountains Press, 1925. Excerpts in *LBTT*

"Apology of Genius." *Dial*, LXXIII (1922), 73–74. *LB* and *LBTT*

"At the Door of the House." *Others: An Anthology of the New Verse (1917)*, ed. Alfred Kreymborg. New York: Alfred A. Knopf, 1917.

"Aviator's Eyes," in Larry Krantz, "Three Neglected Poets." *Wagner Literary Magazine* (Spring, 1959), 52–63.

"The Black Virginity." *Others*, V (December, 1918), 6–7.

"Brancusi's Golden Bird." *Dial*, LXXIII (1922), 507–508. *LB* and *LBTT*

"Café du Néant." *International*, VIII (1914), 255. *LB*

"Chiffon Velours." *Accent*, VII (1947), 112.

"Crab-Angel." *LB* and *LBTT*

"The Dead." *Others for 1919*, ed. Alfred Kreymborg. New York: Nicholas L. Brown, 1920.

"Der Blinde Junge." *LB*

"The Effectual Marriage." *Others: An Anthology of the New Verse (1917)*, ed. Alfred Kreymborg. New York: Alfred A. Knopf, 1917.

"English Rose." (fragment of *Anglo-Mongrels and the Rose*). *LB*

"Ephemerid." *Accent*, VI (1946), 240–41.

"Faun Fare." *Between Worlds*, II (1962), 28–30.

"Hilarious Israel." *Accent*, VII (1947), 110–11.

"Hot Cross Bum." *New Directions 12* (1950), 311–20.

"Human Cylinders." *Others: An Anthology of the New Verse (1917)*, ed. Alfred Kreymborg. New York: Alfred A. Knopf, 1917.

"Idiot Child on a Fire-Escape." *Partisan Review*, XIX (1952), 561.

"Ignoramus." *LB* and *LBTT*

"Impossible Opus." *Between Worlds*, I (1961), 199–200.

"Italian Pictures": "The Costa San Giorgio," "July In Vallombrosa," "Costa Magic." *Trend*, VIII (1914), 220–22. *LB* and *LBTT*

"Joyce's Ulysses." *LB* and *LBTT*

"Jules Pascin." *LBTT*

"Lady Laura in Bohemia." *Pagany*, II (1931), 125–27.

"Lions' Jaws." *Little Review*, VII (September–December, 1920), 39–43.

Love Songs (I–IV). *Others*, I (July, 1915), 6–8. Expanded to *Songs to Joannes*. *Others*, III (April, 1917), entire issue. Excerpts in *LB* and *LBTT*

"Lunar Baedeker." *LB* and *LBTT*

"Mexican Desert." *Dial*, LXX (1921), 672.

"Magasins du Louvre." *LB*

"Negro Dancer." *Between Worlds*, I (1961), 202.

"O Hell." *Contact*, No. 1 (December, 1920), 7. *LB*

"Omen of Victory." *LBTT*

"On Third Avenue: Part 2." *LBTT*

"Parturition." *Trend*, VIII (1914), 93–94. *LB* and *LBTT*

"Perlun." *Dial*, LXXI (1921), 142.

"Photo After Pogrom." *Between Worlds*, I (1961), 201.

"Poe." *Dial*, LXXI (1921), 406. *LB*

"Poem." *Camera Work*, No. 46 (1914), 18.

"Property of Pigeons." *Between Worlds*, I (1961), 203–204.
"Revelation." *LBTT*
"Show me a saint who suffered." *Between Worlds*, II (1962), 27.
"Sketch of a Man on a Platform." *Rogue*, I (April 1, 1915), 12. *LB*
"The Song of the Nightingale Is Like the Scent of a Syringa." *LBTT*
" 'The Starry Sky' of Wyndham Lewis." *LB*
"Stravinski's Flute." *LBTT*
"Three Moments in Paris:" "One O'Clock at Night," "Café du Néant,"
   "Magasins du Louvre." *Rogue*, I (May 1, 1915), 10–11.
"Time-Bomb." *Between Worlds*, I (1961), 200.
"To You." *Others*, III (July, 1916), 27–28.
"Transformation Scene." *LBTT*
"Virgins Plus Curtains Minus Dots." *Rogue*, II (August 15, 1915), 10.
"The Widow's Jazz." *Pagany*, II (1931), 68–70.

PROSE AND DRAMA

"Aphorisms on Futurism." *Camera Work*, No. 45 (January, 1914), 13–15.
Auto-Facial-Construction (pamphlet). Sociétaire du Salon d'Automne.
   Florence: Tipografia Giuntina, 1919.
"Gertrude Stein." *Transatlantic Review*, II (1924) 305–309, 427–30.
"In . . . Formation." *Blind Man*, No. 1 (April 10, 1917), 7.
"John Rodkers Frog." *Little Review*, VII (September–December, 1920),
   56–57.
"O Marcel – – – otherwise I Also Have Been to Louise's." *Blind Man*, No.
   2 (May, 1917), 14–15.
The Pamperers (play). *Dial*, LXIX (1920), 65–78.
"Pas de Commentaires! Louis M. Eilshemius." *Blind Man*, No. 2 (May,
   1917), 11–12.
Psycho-Democracy (pamphlet). Florence: Tipografia Peri & Rossi, 1920;
   reprinted in *Little Review*, VIII (Autumn, 1921), 14–19.
"Questionnaire." *Little Review*, XII (May, 1929), 46.
"Summer Night in a Florentine Slum." *Contact*, No. 1 (December,
   1920),6–7.
"Towards the Unknown" (questionnaire). *View*, I (February–March,
   1942), 10.
Two Plays: "Collision" and "Cittàbapini," *Rogue*, I (August 1, 1915), 15–
   16.

Index